LIBRARY MANAGEMENT

LIBRARY MANAGEMENT

Volume 1

C.K. Sharma
Kiran Singh

ATLANTIC
PUBLISHERS & DISTRIBUTORS

Published by

ATLANTIC
PUBLISHERS & DISTRIBUTORS
B-2, Vishal Enclave, Opp. Rajouri Garden,
New Delhi-110027
Phones : 25413460, 25429987, 25466842

Sales Office
7/22, Ansari Road, Darya Ganj,
New Delhi-110002
Phones : 23273880, 23275880, 23280451
Fax : 91-11-23285873
web : www.atlanticbooks.com
e-mail : info@atlanticbooks.com

ISBN 81-269-0452-6 (Vol. I)
ISBN 81-269-0453-4 (Vol. II)
ISBN 81-269-0454-2 (Set)

Printed in India
at Nice Printing Press, Delhi

PREFACE

Library Management is a complete treatise on the working of library. The book is structured into two Volumes. Volume one comprises chapters on management, organization structure, circulation, library rules, and maintenance and preservation of library material while the second Volume includes operation (productive) management, service management, personnel management, financial management and inventory (maintenance) management.

Beginning with the definition of Management, the first Volume includes in its introductory chapter the objectives and established policies related to Management. Having specialized in the subject and served in the field of Library and Information Science for forty years, we are well-acquainted with all its aspects and procedures; and as such we can assertively say that University Library Management is fully based on Business Management concepts and principles. These concepts are analytically presented in this Volume.

Furthermore, the book presents a detailed study of the various departments — Technical Circulation, Acquisition, and Reference. The special attraction of this Volume is its chapters highlighting the library cooperation, communication and coordination, inter-library loan, budget, and library statistics. Besides these, the extensive informations on Academic Libraries and Public Libraries are highly valuable.

The book seeks to focus on best practices and to offer sufficient insight into the methods and provides valuable guidance to librarians. It will be extremely useful to students, researchers and teachers of Library Science.

It gives us great pleasure to thank all those who have directly or indirectly assisted us in completing this book.

Our special thanks go to Mr. Manish Kumar, CEO, M/s Atlantic Publishers and Distributors, New Delhi, for seeing the Volume through the press.

C.K. SHARMA
KIRAN SINGH

CONTENTS

1

MANAGEMENT

1.1 Definitions

Management means 'the process to manage', the concept of management had been an old one which changed from time to time and reached the modern stage of scientific management. In ancient period, much attention could not be paid to management and was limited to 'public management'. Management also applied to the libraries being a public sector of social welfare.

Scientific management is directly concerned with control, planning and execution of all organized human activities in the different process of library management and thus, profoundly effects human welfare. Its main function is the co-ordination of human activities. Management is quite dynamic and flexible and responsive to changes in the social concepts and economic conditions. A dynamic library enterprise needs top executives of vision, foresightedness and resourcefulness. Management structure is a pyramid, broadest at the base and tapering towards the top. Besides this, every library needs a librarian competent to direct activities in order to put the resources for effective use to achieve the objectives. Library can plan, organize, direct and control the activities of other persons subordinate to him.

Management requires specialized knowledge and expert ability in various fields. It has become a process which acts on the basis of a established knowledge and scientific practices.

Many of the libraries are suffering due to lack of experienced librarians who run the libraries inefficiently. The library should have a man who can command and guide the ship safely. He has a very important role to play in library administration.

Taylor describes that management should take higher responsibility of planning and control with simplified working techniques based on basic principles: (*i*) The development of science for each element of a man's work which well replace the old method of 'rule of thumb'; (*ii*) The selection of the best worker on the scientific basis for each particular task and to retain, teach and develop the worker, instead of old practice of allowing the worker to train himself; (*iii*) Co-operation of the management with the worker and taking the science to them so that all work might be done in accordance with the principles of science which has been developed; and (*iv*) More equal division of responsibility between management taking all responsibility for planning and co-ordination for which it is better fitted.

1.2 Level of Management

There are three levels of management:

(a) **Top Management**: General policies are laid down by the top ranking officials in a management system the (chief) librarian. These are called chief or top executives, who issue necessary orders, instructions and give advice from time to time to their subordinates so as to see that the directions or policies are properly executed for attaining the objectives of the enterprise. They are directly responsible to the library committee about the progress made or the failure of the plans executed by them.

(b) **Middle Management**: There are employers executing and interpreting the policies thoughout the library. Such persons are not the policy-makers but the followers of the policies. They take responsibility of the successful operation of divisions and departments. They are heads of the department divisions. The middle management is an important link in the management structure. They are the persons communicating the orders of the top level to the lower level. Their right interpretation and its implementation can take the library to the high peak of the utility.

(c) **Lower Management**: It includes the supervisory persons. Lower management is also called with the name of 'supervisory management'. The lower management has also got a strong and valuable position in the library because final execution of the policies is carried out by the employees work under their supervision or direction. Lower management is directly responsible to the middle management, office-supervisor and section-supervisors. The lower executive, therefore, acts as the representative of the working staff. In other words, lower management is a link between the middle management and the working staff.

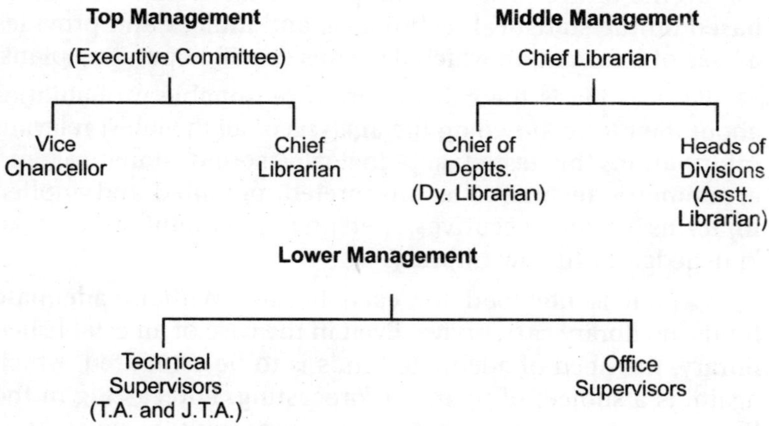

1.3 Planning

Planning involves selecting or establishing objectives and goal and implementing them by means of policies, procedures, rules, programmes and strategies. To get a suitable plan is equivalent to finding out an appropriate characteristics as the basis of classifying entire work cast upon the entire force. Planning and responsibility of planning should be fixed with all supervisors of the library whether they are on the top, the middle, or the bottom of the organization of structure. While we finalize planning decisions, some prerequisites supposed to be considered: (*i*) Diagnosis of a problem; (*ii*) Identification and comparison of possible course by means of rational analysis and allocation of resources and time.

The effective and sound planning leads to growth and progress of the enterprise. Librarians shoulder the responsibility to make planning decisions in such a way that the growth of the library may be developed with its limited resources. Planning thus, becomes a device for change to meet the future. Thus, planning as a function of library is an insightfully visualizing management process of attaining the goal in accordance with the objectives of the library as an organism of social significance.

1.4 Forecasting

Forecasting is nothing more than an estimate of a future condition. One visualizes the future events on the basis of the events of the past and the present facts. The forecast is based on the statistical techniques, and indices and provides a base of information which develops specific operating plans.

Forecasting is the calculation of reasonable probabilities about the future, based on the analysis of all the latest relevant informations by tested and logically sound statistical and econometric technique as interpreted, modified and applied in terms of an executives, personal judgment and social knowledge of his own library.

Capital is lifeblood for each library. Without adequate funds, no library can survive. Even in the case of an established library, the need of adequate funds is to be estimated, which again, is a subject of financial forecasting. Forecasting in the library management has become important because it is essential for various valuable plans and development programmes, leading to an increased correctness in decisions by the management and improved accuracy of policy planning. Forecasting includes the estimates of general conditions and total economy, total demand for the library books and service and scope of providing library facilities.

Forecasts are not fool proof. Every forecast is bound to involve some guesswork about the future. The test for good forecasting is whether it leads to correct management decisions or not. Short-term forecast proves more accurate than the long-term forecasting. On the other hand, assumptions are to be developed logically and the estimation and the assumption together make the future plan. Normally, a programme is prepared for 25 years. The library building should be designed in such a manner that it may not be found short of space during the assigned period.

1.5 Estimated Objectives

Objectives or goals are statements of purposes towards which organising and controlling are aimed and change with the change of conditions or circumstances. While planning a library, objectives are essential. Until and unless objectives are established, the planning cannot be on sound footing. A library might include among it overall objectives a certain rate of service; emphasizing research to develop a continuing flow of library facilities: improving library co-operation, achieving key position among other libraries; adhering to the values of our society. It is believed that a librarian cannot pursue effectively more than a few objectives. Too many objectives before a librarian tend to take the drive out of their accomplishment and many unduly highlights minor objectives to the detriments of major ones.

Objectives will help us to provide individual motivation to those who must fulfil the objectives. It gives direction to the library as a whole; it serves as a basis for co-ordinating staff work, it provides the basis for control, appraisal and results. An academic library has an objective to provide reading facilities to faculty members and the students. Objective may be group goal, intermediate and final objectives, limited and unlimited objectives, elastic and inelastic objectives, external and internal objectives, and long range and short range objectives.

Libraries are supposed to be cultural inherited organs and therefore, the cultural inheritance of society must be reflected through the material possession of library. Hence, every library must try to procure and preserve the cultural documents of the society in addition to the usual reading material. This is the ultimate gain of every library. Henceforth, the objectives of the library must change in accordance with the need and demand of the society for which the library has been established.

1.6 Established Policies

Policies are broad guides to the thinking established to assist subordinates responsible for making plans. Policies delimit an area in which a decision is to be taken and assure that the decision will be consistent with objective.

Policy-making is an essential process in planning. Policies work as a guide to the librarian and stand as a guideline for action to the subordinates to achieve the goal of the library. Policy-making authorities rest with the directors, chief librarians or the library committee and their powers cannot be delegated to any subordinates. Library committee frames policies regarding timings, staffing, appointment, selections and readers service. Librarian frames policy regarding the division of work of subordinates, cataloguing, classification and acquisition. Policies are reviewed periodically by the proper authority to ensure efficient service to the society.

The library is expected to be the centre of knowledge where every reader has the freedom of the mind to think, to discuss and to attain the truth by its intellectual process. The libraries have always been the central agencies for collecting and organizing knowledge for effective use. "The educational system must produce youngman and woman of character and ability committed to national service and development".

The large library is expected to contain research collection, variety of subject books, a large and complex catalogue, reference staff, large building and the open shelf device. The librarian is expected to be a man of fundamental knowledge of the library. He must have general understanding of the means of knowledge, a theoretical knowledge of the library systems, a practical knowledge of the working of the library and a common knowledge of reference tools.

The library was regarded as the sole of any educational institution. Paul Buck presented to the following credo: (*a*) The library is the heart of knowledge; (*b*) Quality faculty is not possible without a quality library; (*c*) Quality education is not possible without a quality library; (*d*) A library is vital to proper exploitation of our intellectual resources; (*e*) A library is essential to maintain free access to ideas and to the functioning of the free mind.

Cyril Norwood has wisely described the importance of library in his address to the ASLIB at Oxford in 1936. "It is better proof of education to know how to use a library than to possess university degree". Library is an important agency to all those who are engaged in research and welfare of the human beings. A library is an important agency to all those who are engaged in research and welfare of the human being. A library is recognized by its collection, reader and the staff. Libraries in India are facing many problems regarding building, finance, staff, furniture and equipment, reading material, classification, cataloguing, reprography, efficient control, reference service and the service conditions of the librarians. Several commissions and committees were set up to discuss these problems but the development of libraries is still on the way.

REFERENCES

Butler, Prince. *Intro. to Library Science.* Chicago Press, 1961.

Christian, N. "Importance of Leadership." *Library Management.* 15, 1994.

Dougherty, R.M. *Scientific Management of Library Operations.* New York, Scarecrow, 1966.

Evans, G.E. *Management Techniques for Librarian.* New York, Aca. Press, 1984.

Howard, Paul. *Library Staff Manuals and a Theory of Library Management.* New York, Cliffton, 1939.

Immelman, R.F.M. *Foundation of Library Management.* Plantiff, Shercon, 1972.

Lowell, M.H. *The Management of Libraries and Information Centres.* Vol. II. Metuchen, N.J., Scorecarew, 1968.

Lowrence, Paul R. *Organizational Behaviour and Administration.* Homewood, Rechard D. Irvin, 1961.

Metcalf, H.C. *Dynamic Administration.* New York, Harper, 1941.

Monday, R. Weyne. *Management: Concept, Practices and Skills.* New Jersey, Prentice Hall, 1995.

O' Conner, M.J. *Research in Library Management.* London, British Library, BLRD Report No. 5550, 1980.

Ranganathan, *Lib. Administration.* Bombay, Asia, 1960.

Sharma, C.K. *Library Management.* Delhi, Shree, 1983.

Shah, Manubhai. "Management by Competence." *Commerce Pamphlet Series.* 1. Bombay, Vora, 1969.

Shull, F.A. *Selected Readings in Management.* Homewood, Irwin, 1962.

Shukla, D.N. "Scientific Management of Libraries." *Library Science Today.* Bombay, Asia, 1965.

Stueart, R.D. *Library Management.* Littleton, Lib. Ltd., 1981.

Taylor, Fredrick W. *Principles of Scientific Management*. N.Y., Harper, 1911.

Urwick, L. *The Elements of Administration*. New York, McGraw Hill, 1969.

Wallace, Joan. *Permissive Management*. New Jersey, Prentice Hall, 1967.

Wheeler, J.L. *Practical Administration of Public Libraries*. New York, 1962.

2

ORGANIZATIONAL STRUCTURE

Generally, all the activities concerned involved in library work and service are called as library work with the business production and library service with the sale of goods in business. Library is a business centre. Many people take business as pleasure and thus to them it is not an end in itself. The main difference between the librarian and the Karta of the family is the financial responsibility. Karta is presumed as a financer and acts as a Business Manager. Hence, Library can be defined as non-profitable business which is a combination of all the characteristics of partnership, joint family and the joint stock company business. Like the business, the library needs to be well organized in order to perform the business of the library effectively. It counts a little whether it is a small or large library because the kind of work performed is the same.

Efficient administration require forecasting and planning in relation to library's objectives, sensible organization and grouping of appropriate activities, calculation of material and personnel requirements. Harrod writes that "the library organization is the set or process of organization, *i.e.* creating a systematic union of individuals in a body whose officials, agents, members work together for a common end." "Organization creates machines and management runs it". Brech has described the organization as the framework of management because it sets our discussion and distribution of the total responsibility into the relevant relations or grouping for more effective performance. Every member of the library is expected to play its role as per the plans chalkout. Brown clearly defines the organization as a part of which each member of an enterprise is expected to perform and the relations between the member to the end that their concerned endeavour shall be more effective for the purpose of the enterprise. Therefore, to make planning effective there must be material and human organization without which no undertaking will be a success.

A library is an institution which accumulates the knowledge and transmits the same to the public and the succeeding generations and exploration of the new knowledge. Libraries are the backbone of the education and hence it requires a efficient organization to serve its readers in dissemination of knowledge. The library organization is a process of establishing the pattern of relationship by assigning duties and responsibilities to each department, section, group and the individual of the enterprise already demarcating the authority, responsibility and duties of each and providing the channel of communication and co-ordination to achieve the objectives of the concern. "Whenever two or more persons work together in a common endeavour, there is need for some division of the work which is the beginning of organization. The activities of even two men require co-ordination to be effective geographically that their activities threw them into intimate relation with each other". Organization is a backbone of library management. All library activities and its functions are grouped under organizational set up. Thus, "the organizational plan can be developed by finding out the proper activities which should be carried out, or grouping them into broad functions; defining precisely the line of authority and the relationship that should exist within and among the units and departments".

2.1 Principles of Organization

(a) **Specialization**: Organizational pattern should have a character of specialization in employees. The work of each person should be confined to a single function. The libraries have different types of technical work *i.e.*, cataloguing, classification, book selection, circulation etc. If a person is entrusted with a single work, it is obvious that the person will become well versed in the task and such type of specialization will be more helpful in a successful organization.

(b) **Unity of direction**: This principle is concerned with the functioning of the body corporate and not with the personnel as in the case of unity of command. Here, there should be no deviation from the plan chalked out in achieving the same objective although there might be different activities. In other words, for achieving the best results, there should be one common plan for the concern as a whole.

(c) **Unity of command**: A worker should not be put under two bosses. Proper work at the lowest cost and in the best manner is possible only if a person is put under the command of one boss. There should be only one supervisor or the officer to supervise over him and the worker should be given the understanding that he is under the command of only one and not many. Under this system there will be no conflict of orders and hence ensures smooth working discipline and jeopardy, and disturbs order and stability of a library. "The unity of command ensures efficiency and quick decisions".

(d) **Delegation**: "Delegation of authority means the shifting of powers to lower authority". It is the conferring of authority from one executive or organization-unit to another. Authority may be delegated from higher to the lower. Hence, authority may be downward. It is not the shifting or transferring of overall or the final authority. The delegator does not surrender his overall responsibility. He retains the power of control. He can ever revoke his delegation and take back all the authority. The chief librarian should take more precautions while delegating the authority. The competence of the person holding the post permanently should be considered. It is also hoped that the librarian should keep the subordinates in regular contact and discuss the problems and guide them. Since the librarian cannot do all the work himself, he delegates powers to his immediate subordinate to enable him to look after certain duties.

(e) **Chain of command (Scalar chain)**: It is a chain which explains the relation between different employees right up from the supervisors enjoying the ultimate authority to the lowest rank. It is a hierarchy of jobs and line of authority starting from the chief executive to the immediate person in subordination and so goes down to the lowest person in the organization. Monney and Reiley have called this hierarchy as scalar principle or the process. This process is also popular with the name of chain of command. Thus "it is the means by which sources are apportioned, persons selected and assigned, operations activated, reviewed and modified".

(f) **Leadership**: Leader serves two purposes: (*i*) The leader guides and motivates the subordinates, (*ii*) Subordinates give him information and responses and modify his behaviour and future plan. Leadership needs drive, intelligence, trust of people, knowledge, human relations, skills etc.

The librarian is a leader of the library staff. A successful leader (librarian) provides four behavioural patterns:

1. Supportive relationship to his followers;
2. Emphasis on attainment of goals;
3. Work facilitation; and
4. Interaction facilitation.

A librarian should have the ability for effective use of groups, managerial assumption about persons and minimum use of hierarchical authority, competence, developing executive, legislative and judicial systems, and psychological understanding.

2.2 Structure

Organization can be divided into two kinds: Formal and Informal. Formal organization is represented by the lines of the establishment authority, such as various supervisors, bosses and staff members. Informal organization is typical by the various contracts and social structure. A business organization is a process of welding together a framework of positions which can be used as a management tool for the most effective pursuit of the goals of library. The library expends its administration will be conducted by specially entrusted persons so as to achieve a high degree of efficiency in day-do-day administration. Lowell suggests that "the organizational structure must be based on some objectives like specialization, unity of direction, unity of command, authority and responsibility, delegation of power, span of managerial authority, chain of command, balance of functions, changing concept etc.".

ORGANIZATIONAL STRUCTURE OF UNIVERSITY LIBRARY

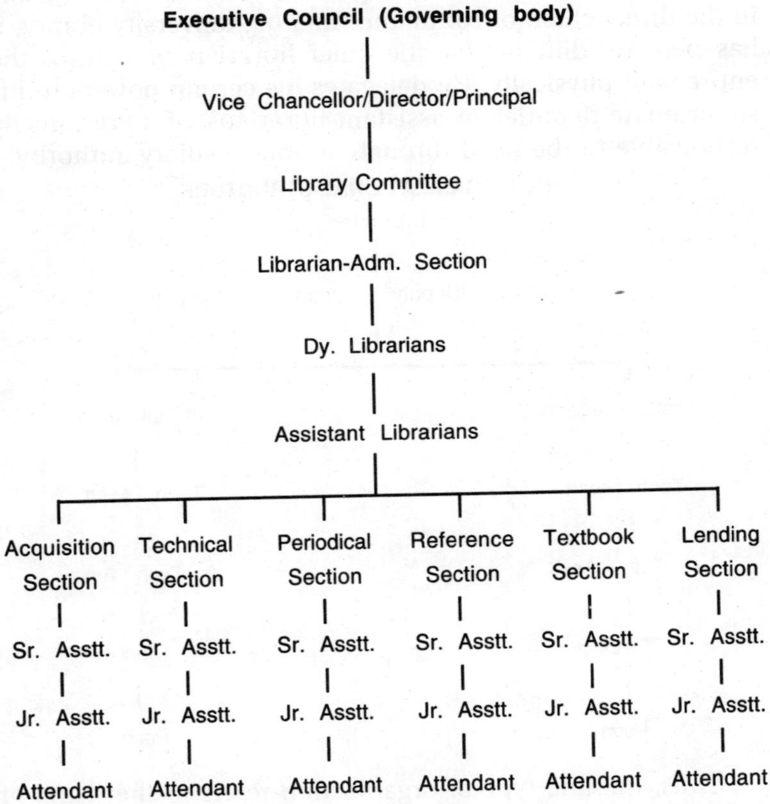

There are three distinct types of organizations have been developed and currently in use:

1. Line organization;
2. Line and the staff organization;
3. Taylor's Functional organization.

2.2.1 *Line Organization*

Line unit denotes the qualitative aspect of organizational pattern. This is the simplest and the oldest type of all organizational forms and popularly called or known as Militate Organization. This type of organization is characterised as by direct line of authority flowing from top to the bottom of the organizational hierarchy and the line of responsibility flowing to an opposite, but in equally direct manner. So, the line type of organization refers to the fixing of authority and responsibility in the direct chain of command. In a big university library, it has become difficult for the chief librarian to control the entire staff physically. He delegates his certain powers to his subordinate deputies or assistant librarians who are directly responsible to the head through an intermediary authority.

LINE ORGANIZATIONAL STRUCTURE

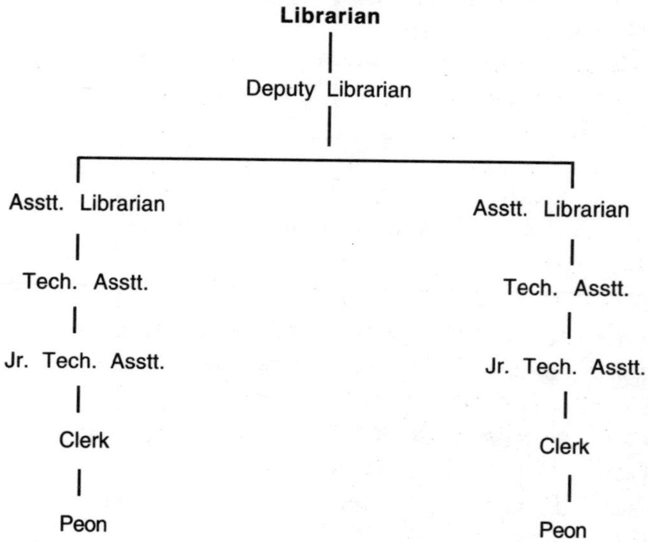

Thus, the line type of organization refers to the fixing of authority and responsibility in a direct chain of command. Each person is directly in-charge of all the people below him and responsible only to his immediate supervisors. Line organization is simple in operation and definite in assigning authority. It gives full freedom to each departmental head; orders are given direct from the boss to his subordinate; every unit is complete in itself. Co-ordination among the different units is a common feature. The line organization method can be successfully practised in small libraries, where methods of operation are straight and simple. Labour problems can be handled easily and routine work is in continuation process.

2.2.2 *Functional Organization*

Organization initiates healthy co-operation among the various wings of the library for their development, recognising the limitations of the line type of organization. Frederick W. Taylor proposed a functional foremanship organization. According to him a foreman must possess the qualities of brains, education, special or technical knowledge, manual dexterity and strength, tact, energy, honesty, judgment, common sense and good health.

The first step in organizing an administrative force as to organize it into convenient sections according to a thought out plan. To get a suitable plan is equivalent to finding out an appropriate characteristics as the basis for classifying the entire work cost upon the administrative force. The characteristics chosen will vary with the nature of the business entrusted to the administration. It may be regional, functional and personal or of any other nature; pure or mixed. Under this plan, the lowest worker in the organization can get the benefit of the services of the specialists who will be performing their functions that are common to different departments under one organization.

Taylor's system of functional organization can be applied to the library as functions and duties of each person in library are divided by the type of the job and the specialization the person has. For example, there are several departments in the university library *i.e.*, Acquisition, Classification, Cataloguing, Reference service and Circulation etc. In this type of organization, all the aspects of a particular job or all the jobs of a particular nature are put together under one head or the supervisor. There will be one in-charge of Technical section, acquisition section, circulation section, periodical section and other departments separately. The supervisor of acquisition section will take the work of the persons attached to him in the same department.

Functional arrangement is usually provided for acquisition, cataloguing, circulation, reference and periodical's departments.

FUNCTIONAL ORGANIZATION

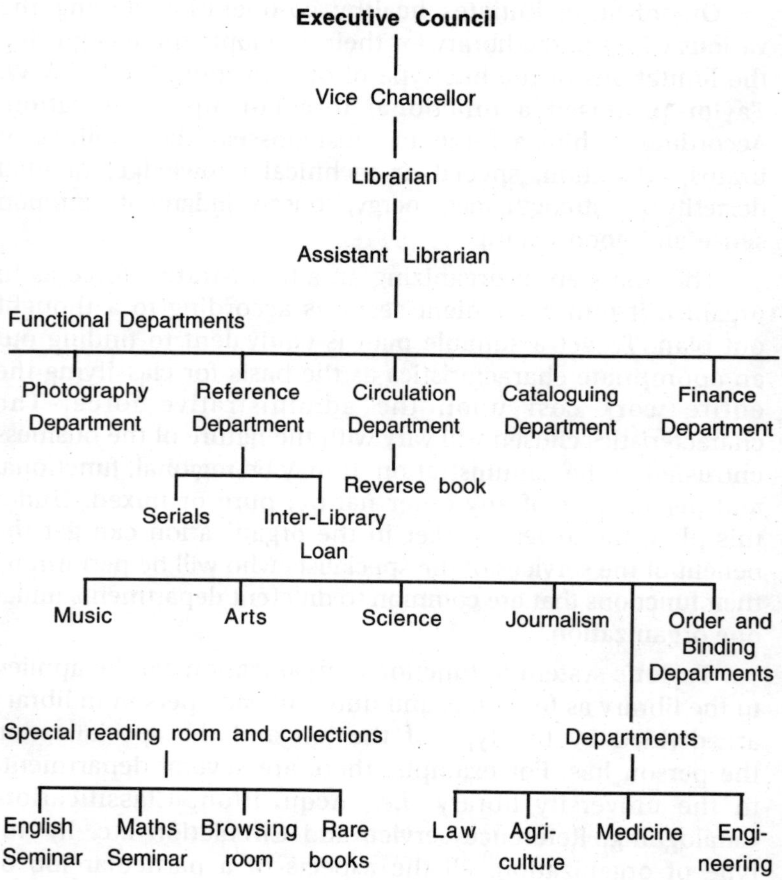

Functional organization consists in so dividing the work of the management that each man from the assistant superintendent down, shall perform as few functions as possible. If practicable, the work of each man in the management should be confined to the performance of single leading function. The most remarkable characteristic of the functional management lies in the contact of the each workman, instead of coming in direct contact with the management at one point only names through, his gang boss, receives his daily orders and help directly from eight different bosses, each of whom performs his and the particular function. Suppose, four of these bosses are in the planning room, and of these three send their orders to and receive their return from the workman, usually in writing. Four others are in the acquisition section, and personally help their men in their work. Each boss helps in his own particular line or function only. Some of these bosses come in contact with each workman for a so short time each day that they can perform their particular duties particularly for all the workman in the acquisition department, and in their line they manage the entire department. Other bosses are called upon to help their men so much and so often that each boss can perform his function for but a few men, and in this particular line, a number of bosses are required, all performing the same function but each having his particular group of man to help.

FUNCTIONAL ORGANIZATION

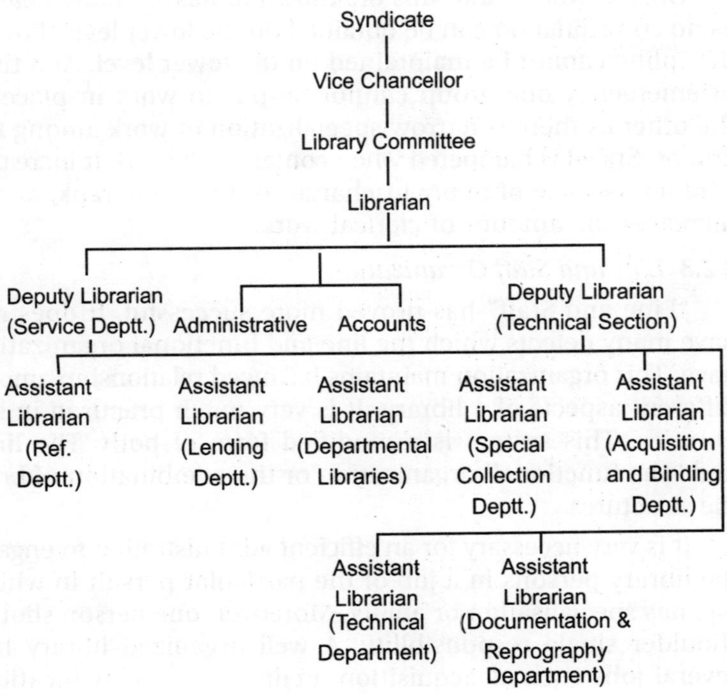

Functional organization has so many merits at its side. It applies, principle of specialization, functions of identical nature, training easily given to supervisors for specialization, facility of machine of capacities and the supervisor's interest, promotion in co-operation, expansion of library, help the workers to undertake intensive study of his work, and better results in library services.

Under this form of arrangement, three individuals report to the librarian, five to the assistant librarian, in-charge of special collection. School libraries has a wide span of control, but direct supervision is usually limited to the special reading rooms and collections and the departmental libraries in the main building. This system is also economical. The librarian, with a reduced span of control, is able to spend more time for planning, promoting faculty library and the student library relationship, making contacts, and engaging in activities of scholarly nature.

On the other hand, this organization has so many defects as no co-ordination can be obtained on the lower level. Proper discipline cannot be maintained on the lower level. At a time of emergency one group cannot be put to work in place of the other as there is narrow specialization of work among the groups. Speed is hampered when contact is divided. It increases conflict because of many in-charges of the same rank, and it increases the amount of clerical work.

2.2.3 *Line and Staff Organization*

"Line and Staff" has proved more successful. It does not have many defects which the line and functional organization have. This organization maintains balanced relationship among different aspects of a library. It is very much practised in big libraries. This system is a modified form of both 'The line' and 'The functional' organization or the combination of both the structures.

It is very necessary for an efficient administration to engage the library persons in a job of the particular persuit in which one has specialisation or ability. Moreover, one person should shoulder single responsibility. A well organized library has several jobs such as acquisition, maintenance, classification, cataloguing, reference, circulation and administration, etc. Some guidelines and the lines of responsibility are to be demarcated for every person. "One officer — one responsibility" should be the principle. A line is fixed for person who may be called as line officer or the section supervisor. "Line and Staff" formula furnishes the best solution for the problems of large libraries. E.W. Smith has described the "line" as under:

(i) It leads to joint responsibility,

(ii) A line officer takes direct action,

(iii) Line officers, though solely responsible and supervisors of their departments, does not give them direct authorities over the line forces in subordinate organization nor does it relieve their line supervisors of the basic responsibility of the results of this work.

(iv) The line organizes the purpose and value of the staff and makes full use of its adviser and assistance.

The Line and Staff organization is having two water-tight compartments; one being that of 'Thinkers' and other that of 'Doers'. Therefore, the staff being the body of the specialists of experts does the functions of the 'thinkers' and the line division does the work of 'doers'. Thus, thinking and doing functions are prudently separated under this system of organization.

Line denotes authority whereas staff stands for advice and counsel. The staff type of administrative organization is supplementary to the line type and it does not serve as an alternative to the latter.

Staff executive is solely concerned with planning, thinking, informing, recommending, and making suggestions, so the staff executive should be quite tactful while making any suggestions or recommendations to the line authority. The "Line and Staff" method is a suitable approach for staff co-ordination. This organization combines the characteristics of the line organization with those of the functional type of organization and thus achieves the advantages of both the type of organizations. In fact, the staff arise from the application of the principle of specialization to the line organization whose executives are responsible for the whole work concerning with their respective department. In other words, the staff officer or the department performs an advisory, co-ordinating and service function for the line.

Line and Staff perform different kinds of functions:

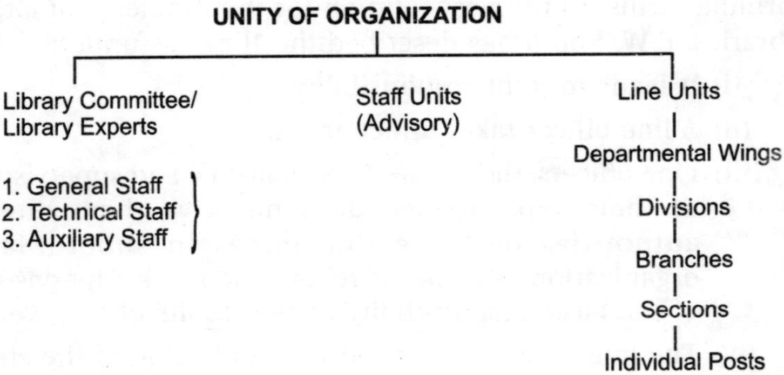

REFERENCES

Appleby, P.H. *Policy and Administration.* Albama University, 1949.

Basu, S.K. *Work Organization and Management Caltt.* Oxford, 1917.

Dunlop, Leslie W. *The Story of Our Library.* Collier's Ency.

Etzioni, Amitai. *Modern Organization.* New Jersey, Prentice Hall, 1964.

Gelfand, M.A. *University Libraries for Developing Countries.* Unesco, 1967.

Harrison, K.C. *First Step in Librarianship.* London, Audul Dentch, 1964.

Jackson, L. *Technical Libraries.* New York, Spl. Lib. Asso., 1951.

Kankle. "Principles of Adm. Organization......" *Coll. & Res. Lib.* 4; 278.

Kinbell, D.S. *Principles of Industrial Organization.* New York, McGraw Hill, 1925.

Lowell, M.H. *Management of Libraries and Information Centres.* Methuchen. Statecrow Press, 1968.

Malinconico, S.M. "Managing Organizational Culture." *Lib. Jrl.* 109, 1984.

Mittal, R.L. *The Library Administration.* Delhi, Metropolitan, 1964.

Porter, L.N. *Behaviour in Organization.* New York, McGraw Hill, 1975.

Shanghnessy, T.W. "Organizational Culture in Libraries." *Jrl. of Lib. Adm.* 9, 1988.

Sharma, C.K. *University Library: Management & Org.* Delhi, Metropolitan, 1977.

Steenkamp, Asidre. "Strategic beplanning." *Cape Libn.* 31, 1987.

Swanson, R.W. "Organizational Theory related to Library Management." *Canadian Lib. Jrl.* 30, 1973.

Wayne State Univ. Lib. *Towards an Assessment of Academic Libraries Organization Effectiveness.* Detriot, Wayne Univ. Lib., 1971.

Wheeler, J.L. *Administration of Public Libraries.* New York, 1962.

Young, H. *Planning, Programming, Budgeting.* Detriot, Gale, 1976.

3

Centralization and Decentralization

Centralization and decentralization has been a matter of controversy and the library authorities have not yet come to a conclusion of agreement as to which of them is suitable. In a library both the systems, centralization and decentralization, are adopted in different situations.

3.1 Centralization

1. Collection of reading material;
2. Library service;
3. Personnel administration.

CENTRALIZATION AREA

Reading material	Library service	Personnel Administration
1. Books	1. Cataloguing	1. Appointment
2. Periodicals	2. Binding	2. Transfer
3. Reprographical material	3. Acquisition	
4. Manuscripts		

Centralization of administration may be used in various degrees depending on the situation. In a library it should not be desirable to have the function of ordering books so decentralized that each department does its own searching, keeps its own records, and makes purchases independent of the other departments. In such an organization there would be expensive, duplication of bibliographical tools, records, and probably book purchased.

Book selection work is also effected by the centralization. According to U.G.C. report "As applied to academic libraries the centralized and decentralized, may refer to the housing of book collection or to the administering of them. The book collection in a university may be housed either in a single repository or in a number of separate depositories. They may be administered as a single unit or as a number of separate units *i.e.* Departmental libraries and Seminar libraries."

German developed departmental libraries for the first time in 19th century and were named as institutes-bibliogheman. "By 1893 there were 114 seminar libraries in Prussian university library." General libraries influenced the U.S.A. scholars and the condition of American libraries was not satisfactory as Henry Bliss says "only Harvard, Yale, Daminount and William universities were having their separate library buildings devoted exclusively to library purposes." Most of the university libraries in U.S.A. has the privilege of centralized book collection as decentralized book selection prevails. The idea of establishment of departmental libraries first came in the mind of Jobus Hopkins who preferred to establish the departmental libraries and central library afterward. Sixteen years late, the same system was inaugurated at Chicago.

3.1.1 *Factors*

There are several factors which effect the centralization.

3.1.1.1 *Geographical area*: In a university whose teaching units are dispersed over a large geographical area or where the university resources should be provided in each unit or departmental library. In such cases copy-right centralization will be absolutely unsuitable. Some special material or services of cataloguing, ordering and binding may be centralized. But "in universities whose faculties and professional schools are controlled in a single area, a number of possibilities present themselves, collections and service can be centralized to a greater degree in the main university library building; easy access to the collection has usefulness to all members of the university community".

3.1.1.2 *Library material*: A departmental library consists of books, journals and other library materials maintained for one or more departments of a university usually housed outside the main library building and administered in one of several different ways.

CENTRALIZED STRUCTURE

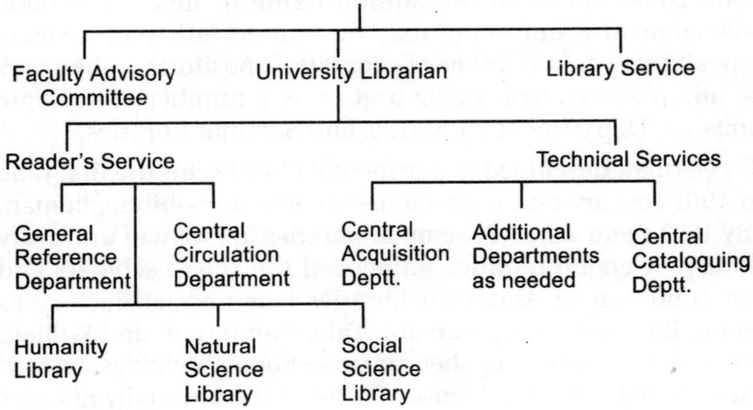

Carl M. White suggested rational decentralization but warned to be more careful while considering decentralization. The solution will vary with local conditions but following factors are to be taken into account:

(i) Combination of low capital costs as well as low costs of operation. On the other hand convenience to all readers. Every separate service point requires: cost of properly equipped space and its maintenance, cost of staff, cost of duplicating material, cost of time and efforts.

(ii) Desirability of decentralization.

(iii) Units of service larger than the one-man library.

(iv) Use of librarian's assistance.

(v) The degree of literature of interest.

(vi) How clear a case can be made for saying that the material cannot be used in the Headquarter library.

(vii) The working habits of specialists in the field.

In the university library the chief librarian usually must deal with such diverse and scattered functions as technical service, reference service, circulation service and departmental libraries. Departmental heads are given freedom to supervise the departmental libraries, subject to the ordinary technical directions of the university librarian. In such a way partial administrative organization can be efficiently run. There are so many disadvantages of complete centralization but more effective in service.

3.2 Decentralization

It is a process of dispersing of authority in number of units. Most of the librarians and the authorities are in favour of centralization, but even then the difficulty arised in administration and the pressure of faculty heads the compelled the circumstances to adopt the decentralized organizational system in universities.

Harvard University of U.S.A. follows the decentralization system on the arguments as follows:

(a) It places the books in convenient locations for those who make the greater use of them;

(b) It broadens the basis of support of the university library system;

(c) It gives the various departments a direct interest in their libraries;

(d) By breaking down the collections into units by subjects, special library methods can be introduced which give better service at no greater cost.

Rational planning is required for rational decentralization and some guidelines should be determined which effect the administration of central universities and departmental libraries. The departmental libraries should be established on the following lines:

(i) The collection should be closely related to the object of the department as funds permits;

(ii) Sufficient physical accommodation should be provided;

(iii) It should have all available literature on the subject most actively needed by the department. Old material should be replaced by newer material from time to time;

(iv) The collection should be freely accessible and provision of supervision of supervisory staff should be considered to ensure necessary accessibility and security;

(v) It should be kept open during normal working hours;

(vi) The library, including staff, space and equipment, should be normal part of regular library system and should be under the supervision of the university library;

(vii) The book fund should be part of centrally administered book budget.

DECENTRALIZATION STRUCTURE

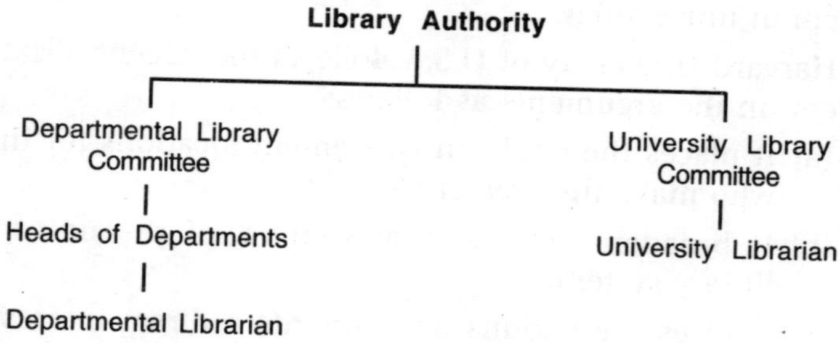

If the authority is dispersed, it is decentralization.

If the authority is controlled, it is centralization.

Having only departmental libraries is not decentralization. The authority to run it, improve it and manage it should also be with the department.

REFERENCES

Bliss, H.E. "Departmental Libraries in Universities." *Edu. Rev.*, Vol. III, 1972.

Sharma, C.K. *Modern Library System*. Delhi, Shree, 1998.

Sharma, C.K. *University Library: Management and Organization*. Delhi, Metropolitan, 1977.

Thompson, James. *An Introduction to University Library Administration*. London, Oliver Bringley, 1970.

4

Departmentalization

Wheeler has clearly mentioned that "Organization of a library department is justified when there emerges as distinct coherent, specialized and important service of at least two persons". Departmentalization is clearly related with the division of labour, the span of control, and the hierarchy. It is a grouping of homogeneous activities under one administrator. Even the Aristotle in his 'Treatise on Politics' has commented on departmentalization that "where the state is large, it is more in accordance with constitutional and with democratic principles that the office should be distributed among many persons". Any action familiarized by repetition is better or sooner performed. It is obvious that as soon as two or more persons combine their efforts towards a common objective, division of work is necessary. It is the primary function of the university library to make books and persons advisory available to its readers. This function is served by two type of departments: Circulation Department and a Reference Department. The former is concerned mainly with the delivery of reading material to its clientele and latter with bibliographic and reference services to students and faculty. Reference section has also separate activities of related nature like, special collection, special equipment such as rare books, maps and music records etc. Such sub-divisions are found mostly in science and technology libraries. Arts and medical libraries also follow it. In every university, the circulation activities are further divided into separate units or divisions such as general loan, reserve books and recreational reading, etc. The divisions have their own heads as clear from the chart mentioned below:

DEPARTMENTALIZATION

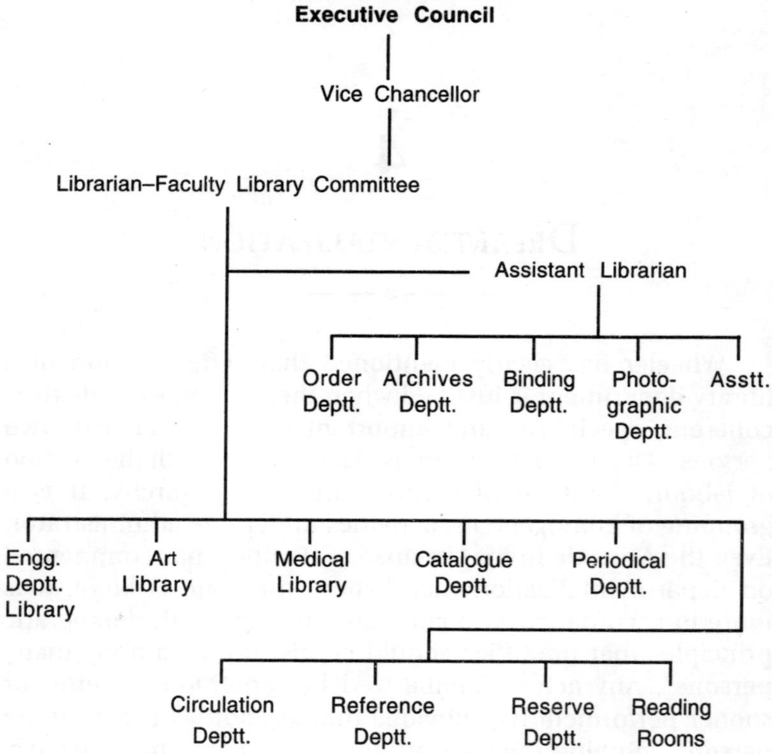

There are still university libraries which are having separate departments for acquisitions, cataloguing and binding. But in modern libraries the trend appears to be in the direction of combining all such activities into a department or division under a single head. Simplicity is worthy goal and past framing and keeping new department at a minimum trend to economy and flexibility.

There are several systems of grouping or departmentalization or sectionalization in university libraries. The important are service section, technical section and the material section. Geographical sections and the undergraduate section may also be separated in order to provide better service and smoothness to library working. Willoughly has stated that "Departmental system is the natural outgrowth of the need of the division of labour in administration and becomes acute when the functions of an enterprize multiply over and over".

Indian National Library has the following departmentalization:

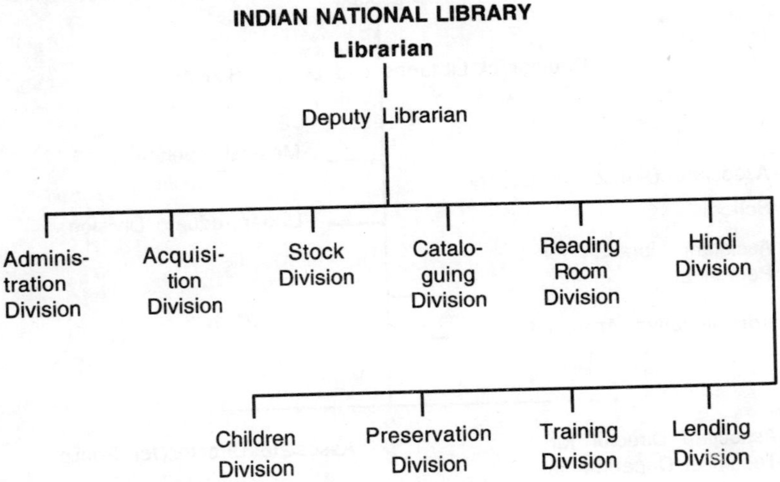

Tauber has divided the functions of university library in two main divisions:

1. Technical Section;
2. Service Section.

There is no uniform pattern of departmentalization in university libraries. The variations are effected by the traditional, personal, physical arrangements, financial availability, curriculum, type of collections, the personality and attitude of library authorities. In recent years there has been some experimentation with departmental organization, and it is likely that this will continue. Department should be generalized on preferential basis if local variables are not involved. University libraries divide the functions of the library and decide a plan of departments. A library may be divided in the following important departments:

4.1 Acquisition Department

It is an important department which acquires the books and the other material more effectively. The standard of

ORGANIZATIONAL CHART OF THE UNIVERSITY OF ILLINOIS LIBRARY AND THE LIBRARY SCHOOL

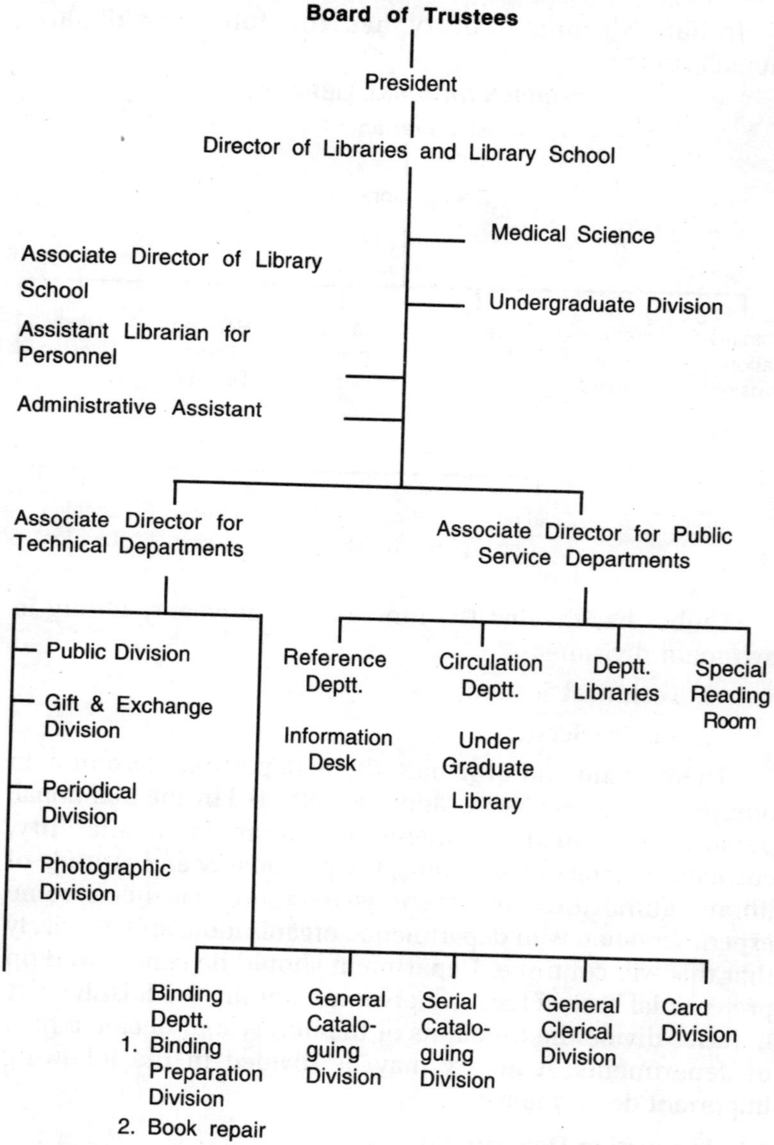

institution is much more evaluated by the acquisition department. This department needs the services of a good administrator who may have a good knowledge of book trade, publishing, as well as the quality to control and supervision and who direct the important business of the unit. Besides an administrator, trained personnels in the field of bibliographies, language and methods are also needed. Acquisition department is enumerated as under:

1. Maintenance of order file, lists, and the records;
2. Maintenance and use of bibliographic aids;
3. Making up, dispatching and filing of orders of books, L.C. cards and other material;
4. Receipts, handling and inspection of incoming shipments;
5. Preparation of bills for payment;
6. Informing individuals recommending the purchase;
7. Ordering and acquisitioning.

In some libraries purchasing is done in the order department. Gifts and exchanges are handled in the order department or in a separate periodical department. Acquisition department should be organized as a separate department and full time workers should be appointed.

4.2 Technical Department

Preparation work includes classification, cataloguing, and mechanical preparation. All these activities are done in the preparation department. But in some big libraries there are separate departments for cataloguing, classification and the mechanical work. No processing department can function effectively without careful planning. Therefore, there should be personnels divided for each type of work. The cataloguing division prepares and maintains the records which reveal the holdings of the library. The operations involved in the preparation of records consists of descriptive, cataloguing, subject cataloguing and classification. Metcalf says "In every library there are types of work that might be assigned to any one of several departments". The important thing often is not to which one they are assigned, but making clear everybody concerned that there is definite assignment.

4.3 Reference Department

Reference department has also separate activities of related nature, like special collection, special equipment, *i.e.* rare book, maps and musical records etc. Such sub-divisions are found mostly in science and technology libraries. A majority of the librarians keep the reference services under reference department. They feel that serials, if treated separately, will cost more. In prevailing practices of most libraries, the operations connected with serial work are distributed among several departments like:

(a) Gift and exchange — In 'order department or periodical department'.

(b) Preparation and cataloguing of serials — In 'Cataloguing department'.

(c) Circulation of serials and assistance for using them — In 'Circulation or reference department'.

The separate departmental system is more effective and provides efficient service. It gives specialized service with its staff persons for specialized fields. Hurt pointed out the requirements and advantages of staff specialization as a means of conserving the interests of the general readers and at the same time rendering service to the specialists.

The extensive use made of periodicals and Government documents of all types in university library has a further bearing on the organization of reference service. There are university libraries in which all work with periodicals and documents are centralised in a serial department. It shows that separate serial's department is responsible for reference service.

4.4 Circulation Department

It is also called as "Loan Department". This department is responsible for the services relating to the loan to the library clientele of books, periodical, maps, music, prints, microfilms and other material. The main object of this department is to maintain a record of loan, recall overdue items. Assesses fine, accepts reserves for books in demand, supplies information for the replacement of books, supervises the arrangement of materials on the shelves.

The organization of circulation section differs from library to library. Organization depends upon the scope of work if this department is centrally organized. A uniform loan practice in all units of library system is adopted. In few universities the circulation division has been expanded into three sections:

(a) Loan Section;

(b) Reserve Bank Section; and

(c) Recreational Reading Section.

Gelfand has classified the main functions of circulation department as to facilitate physical access to library materials and encouragement for its full use, their accurate arrangement on the shelves, and operating on efficient system of loans and returns in accordance with established rules. Circulation department is organised under the supervision of the university librarian. The main organizing activities of this department include identifying prospective borrowers, the circulation process, conducting inventories and searching for missing books, compiling reading lists, assisting readers in use of the library catalogues, assisting students in the selection of books, conducting inter-library loan, maintaining the book stacks, administering a collection of reserved books and other activities.

Local conditions effect the type and numbers of units controlled by the circulation department. While inter-library lending may be the responsibility of one circulation department, in another library it may be handled by the reference librarian. The work may even be distributed between the two units. There are university or other large libraries in India which have separate circulation department for the undergraduate students.

4.5 Reprographic Department

There are few academic and research libraries which have separate photographic department and provide photographic service in a limited manner. Reprographic department includes following activities. Photostating statistical tables for a faculty members, making film strips, answering queries on reproduction of charges, repairing reading machines, advising on the camera, microfilming copies of diaries and other special collection, enlarging photostat etc. The separation of photographic work depends on the types and the purpose of work. If photographic work is undertaken combining with other department it reduces the price, the personnel, the space and the equipment. But on the other hand, if a separate photographic department is established, it will provide more efficient and prompt service though it will cost more. It is necessary to keep this department of good standard and of high quality and as such highly qualified and trained personnels are required. The head of the department wears the responsibility to plan, supervise the work and maintain business procedures. He should be well-versed in preparing photocopying of books, periodicals, manuscripts and other material. In big libraries, the services of photographic department extend beyond the working of micro-production. Photostat, prints, and slides are usually among the other reproducts of the department.

4.6 Serial Department

Periodicals alongwith many documents includes society transactions, serials and other continuation, year books etc. There are important reading material and require active attention. They should be acquired systematically and quickly as they are more useful for reference purposes. Modern university libraries establish serial department as separate department due to the various reasons, *i.e.* availability of trained personnels for serials, minimizing duplicacy of material, regularizing more efficient service, eliminating over departmentalization. This department undertakes all activities pertaining to acquisition, cataloguing, classification, reference work and shelving of serials.

Serials are purchased on annual cost or subscriptions basis which are renewed automatically. Any break in their purchase may lead to difficulty in filling the gaps and frequently may require more funds than if obtained currently.

Serial department provides reference service by giving specific information and guide readers to find facts that can be obtained out of the periodical articles, and provide assistance in the use of indexed and abstracts. Serial department is needed when a large number of serials are collected in the library.

SERIAL DEPARTMENT: An Organizational Chart

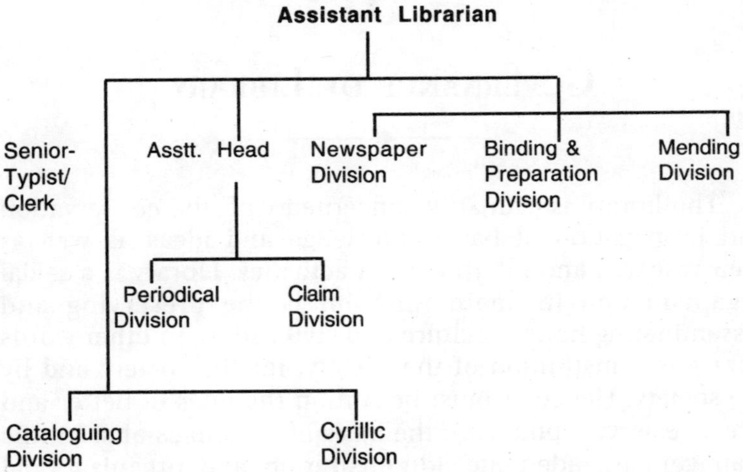

4.7 Extension Department

Large library provide extension service on large scale. Indian university libraries do not generally provide any such service and have not established a separate extension department so far except few universities. Likewise, Delhi and Panjab universities have established extension libraries. But they have not organized a separate Extension department in Central University Library. Extension department includes several functions *i.e.* lectures, forum, radio, and television programme, vocational guidance, debates, lecture series, informal, advisory and demonstration services, dramatic, art and visual activities etc. Large Public libraries services are limited to the campus or city area of university. Under this extension services, library supply reading lists, study outlines and provide inter-library loan, and book procurement service through mobile library van.

5

Governance of Library

The library is primarily concerned with the conservation and propagation of basic knowledge and ideas as well as their research and interpretation activities. Library is a social organism and its main function is the preserving and disseminating human culture and civilization. In other words library is a institution of the society, for the society and by the society. Hence, it must be run on the lines of better and effective service points on the basis of principles of scientific management, adequate administration and organizational system.

The "Government" refers primarily to legal provisions while public library law enacted by state legislatives from the legal basis for the establishment, maintenance and the Government of the public libraries, the university library also would be based on the statutes and ordinances adopted by the Governing body of a university. The statutes made in accordance with the policy enunciated by the university act would determine the status of the librarian in the general set up of the university, and provide for its organization and administration.

5.1 Executive Committee

The Executive Committee is a "executive body of the university. It is a governing body. It has the power to make, amend and cancel ordinances and is responsible for the appointment of university staff (including library) and teachers. It consists generally of nearly 15 persons". As an administrative body, it is concerned with the formulation of general policies of the university library, selection of library officer, appointment of library staff. Generally it appoints the librarian on the recommendation of the selection committee, to whom has been delegated the power of selection of the faculty and many other administrative officers.

5.2 Library Committee

All libraries have library committees. These committees are the Library Committee and the Library Executive Committee. "The decisions of library executive committee are to be finally confined by the executive and the syndicate (Senate)." A library committee is a committee responsible for the management of a library. Library committees are popularly known with several names like 'Library Board', 'Board of Trustees', Board of Directors', 'Library Board', 'Library Advisory Committee', 'Library Management Committee' etc. In nineteenth century there were few libraries who were having library committees. Libraries were run and decisions were taken directly by the head of institution and the librarian. The modern concept of library committee was adopted in the twentieth century. About 69 years ago, there were library committees with administrative powers as librarians were not given proper status. A library committee is now intended to serve in an advisory rather than in an administrative capacity, because the librarians have now been given the requisite status.

"The library committee has been given the freedom only to spread the library revenue in any manner. It likes, subject to provisions in the budget". The location of the branch libraries, the framing of library rules, the appointment of library staff, the policy of book selection and all such internal matters connected with the library are vested in the library committee. Library committee has also vast area of its expansion. It may form its sub-committee for particular problem or activity. For instance, there may be several sub-committees which are limited to the function of book selection. Others may be library finance committee, library administrative committee and maintenance library committee etc. Librarian is the secretary of the committee.

According to survey of Peeler's study, the principles of appointment, structure and form of organization of library committee have been summarized as follows:

(i) The committee should be appointed by the Vice-Chancellor on the recommendation of the librarian;

(ii) It should represent the interest of the library;

(iii) It should be made up chiefly of faculty members;

(iv) The chairman should be a teaching member of the faculty, with recognized qualities of leadership;

(v) The number of members recommended varies from four to ten;

(vi) Membership should be rotated, and terms of the office should be overlap;

(vii) Minutes of the committee should be distributed to the faculty as well as the committee.

5.3 Size of Library Committee

Size: The size of the library committee varies from library to library.

1. Chairman: Number of chairman is always one, who presides over the meetings and is responsible directly to the executive committee.

2. Members: Members are of different types. Members being a faculty head, member nominated by the board, member being a chairman or member of library sub-committee and member by virtue of different posts specified.

3. Ex-Officio Members: The librarian who convenes the library committee works in the capacity of convenor or secretary of the committee.

Duration: Duration of the library committee vary from library to library. Some libraries have permanent committees. Though most of the libraries have advisory type of library committees. Few universities have executive types of library committees. Administrative committees also exist in some libraries.

5.4 Kinds of Library Committee

There are several kinds of library committees:

5.4.1 *Advisory Library Committees*

These committees are also called as recommendatory committees. They have simply advisory powers and their work for the particular problem finishes with the advice of recommendations. "This committee does not have any real power except that these simply recommend certain proposals which are subject to the approval of the library authority".

5.4.2 *Executive Committee*

These committees are most powerful of all the other committees as they have full powers in those matters which are delegated to them. Sometimes this committee needs to report the decision to library authorities. This committee has full freedom to appoint other sub-committees. Executive committee is also known with names of Trustee committee, Management committee etc.

5.4.3 *Ad-hoc Committee*

Such committees are called as special committees which are appointed for specific purposes or for a particular period. They have the statutory authority. This committee works independently.

5.5 Activities of Library Committee

5.5.1 *Administrative*

(a) Planning improvements in the library as a whole in departmental organization and procedures.

(b) Formulating and administering policies, rules and regulations.

(c) Preparing and analyzing reports, statistics, records, graphs, and charts.

(d) Establishing close relationships with faculty, alumni, and readers.

(e) Maintaining official relationship with president, deans, bursar, and others.

(f) Preparing and administering the budget (including book budget).

(g) Directing expenditures, the keeping of financial records.

(h) Making surveys, studies, and analysis of technical and public services.

(i) Planning new buildings and alterations in existing structures.

(j) Seeing that the library buildings and quarters are kept in good condition.

(k) Purchasing supplies and equipment.

(l) Making recommendations regarding appointments, promotions, transfers and dismissals of library staff.

(m) Rating staff members on their efficiency.

(n) Directing the work of the staff.

(o) Approving working schedules.

(p) Classifying the positions and assigning duties.

(q) Discussing personal and professional problems with staff members.

(r) Making the library and its resources known to the student body and faculty through publicity, such as news articles, displays, bulletin boards, talks, special notices, publication, etc.

(s) Directing the inventories made of books, supplies and equipment.

(t) Participating in campus activities, including faculty meetings and faculty committees.

(u) Participating in local, state and national library activities by attendance at meetings, work on committees, etc.

(v) Carrying on professional or research projects.

5.5.2 *Selection and Acquisition*

(a) Reading and evaluating books and other materials

(b) Formulating selection and acquisition policies and procedures for books, serials, documents, pamphlets, and other materials the library may need to acquire

(c) Studying the book and other reading needs of students and faculty

(d) Considering faculty requests for material

(e) Searching records for books and other material requested

(f) Checking the ordering books, checking invoices, etc.

(g) Interviewing salesman, visiting bookstores, book exhibits, etc.

(h) Corresponding the validity of publishers and dealers
(i) Handling gifts and exchanges
(j) Searching for out-of-print items
(k) Setting up and maintaining efficient records in the acquisition processes.

5.5.3 *Provide Guidelines for Preparation of Materials, such as*

(a) Classifying books, serials, ephemeral materials, audio-visual materials
(b) Reclassifying these materials when necessary
(c) Assigning book numbers, subject headings and cross references
(d) Cataloguing non-fiction, fiction, serials, ephemeral materials, audio-visual materials
(e) Searching for cataloguing information
(f) Making master cards, added cards, final revision of cards
(g) Cataloguing
(h) Revising the catalogue
(i) Making added entry cards
(j) Making shelf-list cards
(k) Filing and alphabetizing
(l) Withdrawing from or reinstating books on records
(m) Opening, collating, stamping, perforating, lettering, and shellacking books
(n) Typing and pasting bookplates, date slips, pockets, book cards
(o) Reinforcing pages, making covers, mounting maps, preparing pictures, clippings and miscellaneous materials.

5.5.4 *Framing Rules for Circulation*

(a) Assisting readers to use the catalogue
(b) Explaining arrangement and use of the library
(c) Maintaining borrowers' records
(d) Issuing and receiving books

(e) Preparing reading assignments of the faculty for the reserve shelves

(f) Handling renewals

(g) Filing

(h) Keeping overdue records and collecting fines

(i) Keeping statistics

5.5.5 *Preparing Reference Manual for Reference*

(a) Giving information and answering factual questions

(b) Answering reference questions requiring normal and extended searching

(c) Readers' advisory service-casual and special compiling lists, bibliographies and indexes

(d) Maintaining information files

(e) Borrowing and lending materials on inter-library loan.

Librarian is an administrative head and enjoys following powers —

(a) The librarian, who shall be the Ex-officio member-secretary of the library committee, shall convene the meetings with the approval of the Kulpati/Director/Principal/Chairman.

(b) Subject to the control of the higher authority, the librarian shall bear all responsibilities for the satisfactory administration of the library to the authorities.

(c) Librarian shall formulate and administer policies and regulations for the purpose of securing the best use of the library resources.

(d) He shall prepare and submit to the final authority the annual report of the library by 30th June of each year.

(e) He shall prepare the annual budget of the library and shall also administer all funds allocated in the budget for purchase of books and periodicals or for general purposes of the library with the concurrence of the final authority.

Thus, the librarian shoulders great responsibility of library administration. The efficient functioning of library committee can only be possible with the co-operation of the librarian.

The library committee and the librarian are one and the same. Library is a vehicle, librarian is a driver and the library committee is deemed as fuel. Both are important for the development of the library. Librarian, being the secretary of the library committee calls the committee meetings, performs the duty of reporter in meeting, prepares the proceedings of the meeting and submits it to the higher authority for the perusal and approval of executive committee. An efficient librarian always systematises his work in relation to the committee both before the meetings and after the meetings in giving effect to its decisions.

AREA OF LIBRARY COMMITTEE

1. Library budget
2. Branch libraries
3. Maintenance (Expansion of accommodation, maintenance of building)
4. Purchasing (tendering & selection of books)
5. Staff problems (appointment, staff requirement and staff problems)
6. Library service (lending departmentalization, reference services)

In some large library, authorities delegate all controlling powers to library committee. Its constitution is determined by the higher governing bodies like syndicate, senate, executive council, or the court or board of trustees. The library committee of few University controls the academic policy of the library and exercises the following other functions:

1. It shall have power to re-appropriate funds from one budget head to another within the budgeted allotment;
2. The library committee shall determine the number, nature and salaries of the officers of the class 'B';
3. The committee shall be competent to take such disciplinary action including fine, stoppage of the annual increments, as it may think necessary against any officer of class 'B' and the menial establishment in case of serious neglect of duty or misconduct. The members, so affected may, however, appeal to the

syndicate as prescribed by the regulations relating to appointment etc.

4. The libraries shall be under the orders and control of the library committee in all matters connected with definitions and discharge of his duties.

In practice the Chairman/President is responsible for such selection. Successful practice indicates that the responsibility is one which should be assumed by the chairman and representation on the committee should be carefully served. Student or readers body should also have representation on the committee should be carefully served. Student body or readers representatives should also have representation in the library committee. Since well qualified and trained librarians manage the libraries, the committee should only be of advisory nature and it should suggest only about the library service. Book selection work, which has been one of the important function of the committee, should be left to the chairman, board of studies, Head of departments and the librarian. In case the committee have the executive powers, the librarian has to run to the library committee for each problem and its decision. It results in the interference and creates obstacle in the growth of the library.

The committee pattern of library government is losing ground because it is no longer well adapted to the purpose. It was well suited to pioneer conditions when universities, libraries or large libraries were small units and the library management had little time and no special skill. It has also been used with varying degrees of success as a bureaucratic device for protecting the library from the incompetence of a librarian who was too weak for his job.

LIBRARIAN

In past the library was only a depository of written and printed records and the librarian was simply a collector or the man who was made for getting, assembling and housing the books. In modern age librarian is chief executive of the library. He is solely responsible for the internal discipline and arrangements in the library. The librarian plays an important part in the library committee also. A library committee is responsible for policy making while librarian has to implement it in rigid manner and within the framework of the general policy of the committee. He plays the part of the advisor and also of the executive depending partly on the personal quality of the librarian and in part also on the tradition of the university. Rutgers university in its status has defined, "The librarian of the university shall have general supervision of all libraries...". Since the inception of the new developments in librarianship during twentieth century, university librarians have been vested with full administrative powers. Their status and pay scales have been fixed at par with teaching departments.

Library is a vital organ of the (library's authority) academic, special and public organizations and that he who directs its policies to potentially second in importance only to the president as custodian of the institution's well-being. In the eyes of Ravindra Nath Tagore "The worth of a librarian should be gauged by his power of attracting and looking after such circles by acting as the intermediary of an intimacy of relationship between reader and the library". D.J. Fosket an eminent librarian has expressed his thought about the value of a librarian in the following lines:

"Everyman I will go with these and be thy guide,
In the most need to go by thy side.
And everyman's answer is my answer too.
In good condition I am now in every thing"

and on the whole, content with this good thing. Librarian unifies and correlates library programmes.

The librarian performs the following important functions:

1. *General function*: To seek and cultivate new knowledge, to engage vigorously, fearlessly in the pursuit of truth, and to interpret old knowledge and beliefs in the light of new needs and discoveries.
2. To provide the right kind of leadership in all walks of life, to identify gifted youths and help them, develop their potential to the full by cultivating physical fitness, developing the powers of the mind and cultivating right interests, attitudes, moral and intellectual values.

3. To provide society with competent men and women trained in agriculture, arts, medicine, science, technology and various other professionals, who will also be cultivated individuals, induced with a sense of social purpose.
4. To strive, to promote quality and social justice and to reduce social and cultural differences through diffusion of education.
5. To foster in the teachers and students and the public and through them in society. Generally the attitudes and values needed for developing the "good life" in individuals and the society.

There are four kinds of services which the librarian can render:

1. He can assist all members of faculty in planning for the acquisition of the material to support their activities.
2. He can keep them informed concerning the reference and bibliographic services of the library and the use of the material.
3. He works with members of library staff whose competence justifies it. He may participate in conducting the courses in bibliography and source material in special fields, open to readers beginning lower graduate study and engaged in advanced study and research.
4. He can co-operate with other librarians, with representatives of the faculties of other institutions, with foundations and learned societies and with government agencies and research bodies in carrying out co-operative understanding the object of which is to increase the service of the libraries to scholars everywhere.

"A librarian is the inner wheel of informal education. Librarian must be acquainted with total educational programme of the organization and must be able to adjust its administrative capability to those of the institute".

REFERENCES

Arthur, D. *Guideline for Effective Management.* Sup. Mangt., 24, 1979.

Barnard, C.I. *The Functions of Executive.* Cambridge, Harvard University Press, 1938.

Burby, R.J. *Intro. to Basic supervision of People.* Massachusetts, Add. Wesley, 1966.

Christian, N. "Importance of leadership." *Library Management.* 15, 5, 1994.

Drucker, P.F. *Management: Task Responsibilities.* Bombay, Allied, 1975.

Foskett, D.J. "The Creed of a Librarian." *Lib.-Asso.*, 1962.

Foskett, Johud. "Do you get Maximum Benefits from your Executive Meetings." *Int. Management.* Jan. 1966.

Kay, Brain R. *Challenge of Supervision.* New York, McGraw Hill, 1961.

Lorsch, J.W. *Studies in Organizational Design.* Homewood, Rechard D. Irwin, 1970.

Luthans, Fred. *Organizational Behaviour.* Tokyo, McGraw Hill, 1981.

Mangla, P.B. *University Libraries and Librarians in India.* University News, 30, 1992.

Marchant, M.P. *Participative Management in Academic Libraries.* Westport, Greenwood, 1976.

McCarthy. "Advisory Committee of Administrative Boara. Coll. & Res. Lib. Committee." *Lib. Qrly.* XXI; 120-26.

Nanda, V.B. "Students Participation in Univ. Libraries." *Ind. Lib.* Dec. 1974.

Radcliffe, F.W. *Committees and Librarianship.* Libri., 22, 1972.

Selwin, H.C. *The Effect of Leadership.* Illinois, Free Press, 1960.

Sharma, C.K. *University Library: Management & Organization.* Delhi, Metropolitan, 1977.

Sharma, J.S. *The Substance of Library Science.* Bombay, Asia, 1965.

Young, V.G. *Library Trustees.* New York, Bowker, 1978.

6

Technical Department

6.1 Planning and Policies

The 'proportional processes' classification, cataloguing, and mechanical preparation are the main technical aspects of library work. The catalogue is roughly the record of the holdings of one library and is a guide to the identification and location of each item on the shelves.

The technical department prepares and maintains the records which identify and locate the holdings of the library. It has ordinarily the responsibility for cataloguing and classifying books, periodicals, newspapers, and other serials, pamphlets, documents (govt. publications), manuscripts, films, phono-records, music etc. The product of the department consists of necessary records for the public catalogue, the official catalogue, the shelf list, special catalogues and other catalogues for departmental libraries.

In small libraries, the acquisition and cataloguing work have been brought together in a single department, and, occasionally, binding has been combined with these processes. In the average library, however, where the relatively small staff makes it feasible for the librarian to keep in close touch with the work of all departments, it is quite possible to attain these benefits without adopting this particular plan of organization.

The process carried on in the technical department have as their general purpose the incorporation of books and other library materials into the classified and catalogued collections of the library. If the library organization is large enough to make possible a separate cataloguing staff, it becomes the duty of the librarian to decide which operations relating to this general purpose are to be carried on by this staff. Librarian must establish certain broad policies relating to the work and personnel of the department.

To the in-charge technical section should be delegated the authority and responsibility for such matters as follows: formulating and recommending policies which are the concern of the technical department but which also effect work of other divisions of the library; giving advice on:

(a) policies effecting the technical department,

(b) planning the departmental budget,

(c) selecting the departmental personnel,

(d) making decisions about departmental transfer,

(e) working schedules,

(f) work assignments,

(g) other personnel matters.

All such policies should be determined in accordance with general policies regarding —

1. formulating and directing departmental routines and practices,
2. within the limits of general library policy.

However, the librarian must decide which of the several technical operations are to be performed in the technical department. It is also a common practice to assign to this department the mechanical preparation of books for the shelves.

The librarian must make the decision whether the cataloguing of books for these libraries is to be done by the staff of each departmental library or by the cataloguing staff of the general library. The principal point made by those favouring decentralized cataloguing is that it makes possible better adaptation of classification and cataloguing, particularly subject headings, to the special needs of the users of the departmental library. It makes for economy and a good quality of work to have all persons doing cataloguing organized in one group so as to give the largest opportunity for differentiation and specialization. The advantage claimed for decentralization can be secured to a high degree under the centralized plan by proper co-ordination between the general catalogue department and the departmental library.

The technical department shares with the other departments the library's responsibilities in the library programme. Consequently, it must co-ordinate its efforts effectively with these departments. Like reference work and circulation work, cataloguing is essentially a service function. The better the service rendered by the technical department to the reference and circulation departments, the better can be the service rendered by these departments to the community. Cataloguers should be eager to receive such helpful information. By making wise use of such knowledge yet without yielding either its authority or responsibility, the technical department can develop a catalogue and a classified collection which will serve most effectively the needs of the readers/users.

6.2 Division of Work

The division of work in a technical department is likely to proceed along various lines. The principle of work division which takes into account the differences in training and experience of the personnel is too well recognized to require elaboration. There may also be division on the basis of departmental functions, and, in the case of the professional staff, on the basis of subject, language, or type of material.

Division along functional lines will separate the clerical from the technical processes. Such technical operations as classifying, assigning of subject headings, descriptive cataloguing, and revising may be divided among individuals or groups making up the cataloguing staff.

The extent to which the work of the technical department can be divided depends chiefly on the size of the staff. As the number of staff members increases, problems of organization and work division inevitably become more complex. The head of the technical department is quite likely to find the solution to these problems by using a combination of two or more schemes of division, that is, by function, subject, language, and type of material.

Furthermore, the staff should have a working knowledge of classification and cataloguing procedures and of the uses of catalogues, bibliographies and book lists; a knowledge of modern library organization, procedure, policy, aims and service, particularly as they relate to cataloguing; a knowledge of books; a reading knowledge of one or more foreign languages; skill in the performance of cataloguing; and an appreciation of the objectives and procedures of higher education. The personal qualities desired for one holding this position include: accuracy, good judgment, orderliness; resourcefulness; ability to organize work; ability to follow instructions; ability to get along well with superiors, co-workers, and subordinate.

The in-charge librarian of technical department has charge of a department and is responsible for laying out and assigning the cataloguing and related work for other members of the staff and for seeing that they are effectively employed; assisting them with their difficult problems; developing the catalogues and the cataloguing procedures to meet the needs; cataloguing, classifying and assigning subject headings; supervising and handling processing details; seeing to it that the necessary bibliographical tools and mechanical equipment are available for the work of the staff; making recommendations and decisions in matters of cataloguing policy; maintaining a manual of departmental routines; seeing to it that essential records and statistics are kept; preparing reports and memoranda; handling correspondence; consulting with chiefs of other departments; making recommendations regarding staff appointments, promotions, transfers, salary adjustments and other personnel matters; and attending to other duties of a similar character coming within the scope of the technical department.

The most difficult clerical work is to be done by the Catalogue Assistant working under the supervision of a member of the professional cataloguing staff. Typical duties to be performed by this clerk include: instructing clerical workers in the lower grades; assisting in laying out and assigning their work; typing complex cards from copy supplied; shelf-listing; filing and supervising filing; changing records for items added or withdrawn; and doing other clerical work of similar difficulty.

In small libraries technical department is run in a big hall or in Librarian's room, while in his libraries the technical department is housed in separate wing, section or room.

The best location of cataloguing department is somewhat complex. The department should be close to bibliographical and biographical collection of reference tools maintained for the convenient use of cataloguers serves simultaneously the needs of order assistants. So far as circumstances permit, however, the department should be located conveniently atleast with respect to the public catalogue, the order department, and the reference room.

6.3 Cataloguing and Classification

The principal items of furniture in the departments are desks, work tables, chairs, and book trucks. Card cases will need to be provided to hold one or more of the following official records: (1) the shelf list, (2) the official catalogue, (3) the name authority file, (4) the subject heading authority file, and (5) the record file of material "in process". Sufficient wall shelving should be installed to facilitate efficient routine and handling of books. All equipment should meet the standards of material and workmanship maintained by the established manufacturers of library furniture.

Unless they are required to make typewritten process or copy slips, cataloguers do not need typewriters themselves, but the clerical assistants responsible for typing catalogue cards, or for adding call numbers and headings to unit cards, will require standard typewriters equipped with the special library keyboard and a card holding device. For duplicating unit catalogue cards, the special equipment necessary for carrying on whatever method of duplication has been adopted must be supplied.

Books are the professional tools for cataloguer. Some of these tools — classification tables, cataloguing rules, subject heading lists, special departmental rules and routines are so constantly referred to that copies must be either on each cataloguer's desk or within convenient reach. Cataloguers should find, an English language dictionary, copies of the most needed bi-lingual dictionaries, essential biographical dictionaries, style manuals, filing codes, classification schemes etc.

The technical department will receive from the order department all library materials which are to be processed. The catalogue librarian will need to establish a routine which will regulate the distribution and routine of material through his department. In developing this routine, he will have to take into consideration the following points: (1) books to be accessioned will have to be separated from material not to be accessioned; (2) books urgently needed must be given precedence in every operation over others not in immediate demand; (3) division of the material according to the kind of cataloguing treatment it is to receive is necessary; and (4) routine must be planned with respect to the logical sequence of operations and the personnel which is to perform them.

Most of the processes covered by the terms cataloguing and classification need to be done by trained cataloguers, but some of the simpler and routine operations may be done by clerical assistants working under the supervision of a cataloguer. Clerks, for example, may do the preliminary searching in the catalogue to identify added copies or different editions as well as the form of entry for new books by authors already represented in the catalogue. They may also do all except the more difficult shelf-listing. The extent to which work of this type can be assigned to clerical workers will depend on the amount of such help which is available and the ability and experience individual clerks bring to the job.

Although many library classification systems have been devised, a realistic approach to the problem as to which system to adopt for use.

Once a classification system has been adopted, it is necessary to establish the special policies which are to govern its application and interpretation in the particular library. In the case of the decimal classification, it will be necessary to determine how close the classification needs to be in its many divisions. The decision must be based chiefly on the size of the books collection and the probable future expansion of its principal divisions, but it will be influenced also by the question whether or not users are to have direct access to the shelves.

They are two current printed lists of subject headings namely, the Sears list and the Library of Congress list. Although the Sears list is very good and well suited to the needs of the small library, college libraries will probably find it advantageous to base their subject heading work on the Library of Congress list. The arguments favouring the use of this list are reinforced by the following considerations: (1) three separately issued auxiliary lists may be used effectively with the general list; (2) the tracings of the subject headings on Library of Congress cards simplify subject heading work; (3) the cumulative supplements to the list contribute greatly toward keeping subject heading work up-to-date.

That part of the cataloguing process which relates to the identification and bibliographic description of books, as distinguished from the processes of classification and assigning of subject headings, is called descriptive cataloguing. It involves the making of a copy or process slip which, after the call number and subject headings are added, contains all the information needed for cataloguing a title fully.

Consistency and accuracy in a catalogue are so important that final revision of the cataloguer's and classifier's work is an accepted part of the routine in most libraries. The work of revision requires competence in all phases of cataloguing work and familiarity with the cataloguing and classification policies of the particular library. Considerable judgment and discretion on the part of the reviser are needed to keep in check a tendency toward devoting a disproportionate amount of time to revision. Careful and detailed revision of a cataloguer's work should not be continued after he has demonstrated his accuracy, ability, and knowledge of library policies. This process involves assigning to a newly catalogued title a distinctive call number and making and filing a temporary or permanent shelf card. In some libraries, the original order card is made into an official shelf card.

Shelf-listing is done in some libraries by the cataloguer as a step in the preparation of the copy slip. However, since the author number is normally based on the main entry, many libraries think it more logical to have this process come after the copy slip has received the approval of the reviser.

6.4 Reclassification and Recataloguing

A certain amount of reclassifying and recataloguing is a normal routine of every library. Only a relatively small part of this work involves the correction of errors. It is required by the unforeseen growth of the classification scheme or its revision. In most libraries, routine recataloguing is made necessary in part by old entries which are inadequate for present needs, but most of it occur when changes are made in the name of personal or corporate author.

It involves cost of labour and material. Hence careful considerations should be made to the following questions —

1. Whether the classification system has deficiency?
2. Whether reorganization of library affects the cataloguing?

With respect to methods of procedure for carrying out the project, the plan should make definite provision for the necessary staff, working quarters, and equipment. It should outline the general policies as to (1) the extent and kind of recataloguing; (2) the use of subject headings; and (3) the application of the new classification system. It should include decisions regarding the essential library records involved in the project. It should determine the order of work by classes and establish the policy which is to govern the treatment of current acquisitions. And, finally, it should provide routines covering the mechanical processes.

More libraries have adopted a process involving the use of a stencil duplicator, such as the Dick mimeograph which is especially adapted to the reproduction of catalogue cards. Most stencils can be cut with a standard typewriter equipped with the special characters most frequently needed in catalogue entries.

Libraries which, in addition to the general catalogue, maintain departmental catalogues and other extra files, and which furnish copies of their catalogue cards to the union catalogues of the Library of Congress and other institutions, can use multigraph equipment efficiently. It is possible to obtain multigraph characters in various type faces as well as fonts of the more important non-Roman alphabets.

6.5 Filing

The filing of cards into the library catalogue, shelf-list, and other card records is essentially technical function, but it demands the closest supervision until the filer is thoroughly familiar with the filing rules and has attained such a degree of accuracy as to make further supervision unnecessary.

The filing process is generally accomplished in two steps. First, all the cards to be filed into the catalogue are arranged according to the official filing rules; following this they are filed into the catalogue.

In some libraries, an intermediary step is interposed in the filing process. After the cards are first arranged, they are filed into a file supplementary to the card catalogue proper. This supplementary file is allowed to grow until it is economical to file these cards into the main catalogue. Since this practice places the emphasis on economical procedure rather than on service to readers, it is not to be recommended.

REFERENCES

Adams. "Divided Catalogue in Practice." *PNLA Qrly.* 7; 49-50.

Austin, N.P. "The Newspaper Library." *Spl. Lib.* 41, 1950.

Coney, Donald. "The Administration of Technical Process" in current issues in *Lib. Administration.* Chicago Univ. Press, 1939.

Jackson, L. "Technical Libraries." N.Y., *Spl. Lib. Asso.*, 1951.

Joseph, R. "Library of Newspapers in Kerala." *Int. Lib. Rev.* 23, 1991.

Redmond, D.A. "Small Technical Libraries." *Lib. Qrly.* 34; 1964.

Sharma, C.K. *University Library: Management and Organization.* Delhi, Metropolitan, 1977.

Technical Services Division in Libraries. *Coll. & Res. Lib.* 10, 46-48.

Wilson, L.R. and Tauber, M. *The University Library.* Chicago Univ., 1945.

Wilson, L.R. "A Description of Technical Services Division in Large Libraries." *Coll. and Res. Lib.* Jan. 1949.

7

Circulation Department

Circulation work is not merely a routine business of handling out books at a loan desk or of keeping records of library use. It is the nerve center of the library, the point at which readers and books are brought together. The working of the department touch human beings, not materials, with forces that sometimes lie outside the control of the library staff. Such circulation work implies not only large responsibilities but even greater privileges; the opportunity to introduce readers to books; to make friendly, personal contacts with readers and to make library work not simply a mechanical service but an educational force. Consciously or unconsciously, everyone connected with the library performs the functions of circulation work. These functions are: (1) to secure promptly all books requested by readers; (2) to substitute when possible suitable and adequate material if the desired book or books are not available or are charged out; (3) to assist readers in using the card catalogue and to impress upon them the importance of the catalogue as a key to the resources of the library; (4) to help readers in finding information through general reference books, such as encyclopedias and statistical handbooks; (5) to become acquainted with readers their interests, library problems, and capacities; (6) to direct readers in the selection of books for general reading through personal guidance and planned exhibits; and (7) to interpret the library through friendly and efficient service to all its users. The circulation staff has an important liaison function between readers and books. Success in carrying out its functions will depend on an understanding of the educational function of the library, careful planning and organization of circulation duties, genuine interest in and ability to meet all types of readers, and a wide knowledge of books.

7.1 Organization

Effective circulation service requires a workable organization. The library is vitally concerned with making available to readers material. Therefore, provision should be made for taking care of assigned readings, of recommended supplementary material, and of the general book collection from which students draw their information and materials for individual investigations. Books housed in the reserve room are used principally in the library building because the demand for them is so great that they cannot be circulated for the long loan period. The use of the general collection is serviced through the main loan desk, through the reference department, and through other divisions, depending on the size of the library and the method of handling special materials, such as microfilm, pictures, and phonograph records.

The organization of circulation department must also take into account the manner of dividing the work among members of the staff. In the small library the service to readers centers at the loan desk and the work is done by the librarian. As the library grows, the librarian finds that he must delegate to full-time assistants those parts of the work that exceed his capacity. At first he delegates the duties to the assistants but assumes the responsibility for their supervision; then, when the work of supervision becomes too great in volume, he sets up a circulation department with a supervisor in-charge.

In circulation work there are three places where duties may be divided: (1) the Loan desk, (2) Reserve room, and (3) the Recreational room. The head of circulation is in-charge who is responsible to the librarian. The in-charge of circulation department plan and supervise the work of the circulation staff; develop procedures to meet the needs to discuss circulation problems and policies with the librarian; study the needs of members and to inform them about available material; assist with the instructional service at the loan desk; handle difficult situations and to adjust their complaints; make recommendations for duplicating titles in demand, replacing or rebinding worn volumes; and see that essential records and statistics are kept properly for library use.

The satisfactory handling of a reader's request may mean help from several departments and from staff members doing different but related kinds of work. The mechanics of handling and circulating materials tend to multiply as the size of the library increases. If the circulation assistant were responsible merely for charging book, perhaps he would not understand how his work affects the service of the library as a whole and circulation work cannot be done without an understanding of the whole situation. Because of the cumbersomeness and overlapping of work in a system of many different divisions, some librarians have found it desirable to center all duties relating to readers in a separate readers' division.

7.2 Classification of Professionals

The difficulty of classifying professional is perhaps greater than in other phases of work because of the conditions under which these duties bring staff and readers together.

The classification of work and the assignment of duties in one library, having a circulation staff of four full-time professional assistants.

Professional Duties	*Responsible Person*
1. Decisions on matters of policy	Head of circulation department in consultation with the librarian
2. Instructional relationships with students: Assistance in using the card catalogue Guidance in the selection of books Quick reference service Conferences with students	Head of circulation department
3. Instructional relationships faculty: Conferences on individual readers need Consultation on the book replacement and duplication Location of material	Head of circulation department

(*Contd.*)

Professional Duties	Responsible Person
4. Supervision of the loan desk	Head of circulation department and circulation assistant
5. Reserve room supervision	Reserve librarian/circulation head
6. Supervision of fines and over dues	Circulation Head
7. Keeping records and statistics on library use	Circulation Head
8. Supervision of stacks	Head of circulation department
9. Sending out books on inter-library loan to other libraries	Reference Head
10. Preparation of annual and special reports of the department	Dy. Librarian
11. Preparing exhibits and displays	Dy. Librarian

Clerical Duties	Staff-Responsible
1. Delivery of books from stacks to the loan desk	Library attendants
2. Charging and discharging library materials	Library assistants and all members of the professional staff
3. Arranging and filing cards for current circulation	Library assistants and all members of the professional staff
4. Renewing books	Library assistants and all members of the professional staff
5. Collecting fines and making fine records	Library assistants
6. Checking for missing books	Library assistants
7. Sorting and shelving returned books	Book Lifter

The circulation staff is responsible for giving continuous service to readers during the hours the library is open. In order to provide this service a regular schedule is necessary, with the hours of the professional staff. It is in the interest of staff's morale to divide the work fairly, taking into account, of course, personal qualifications, experience, and training, and to consider individual preferences for hours of work as long as it can be done in fairness to all.

Most librarians agree that a trained librarian should be on duty every hour the library is open. If the staff is small and if the library is open for a long period of time, it will probably be necessary to leave an experienced assistant in-charge of the loan desk during slack periods. In preparing individual schedules for the professional staff, an effort should be made to relieve the strain caused by long hours at the loan desk by assigning to each person special duties worthy of the staff member's particular interest and ability.

If the library is kept open during vacation and holiday periods, the arrangement of schedules must be made in such a way as to insure the best service while giving the staff the fullest benefit of the holidays to which it is entitled. Summer vacations are usually staggered during May, June. Although it is important to have a trained staff member in-charge during the Christmas and spring holiday periods, compensation for this duty should be time off directly before or after the holiday period. The assignment of holiday work should be distributed fairly to all staff members according to a definite schedule.

The circulation staff is responsible to serve quickly and easily. To do this requires an efficient charging system which will show: (1) what books are charged out to readers and where books are that are not in their proper place on the shelves; and (2) when books charged to readers are due for return. Some libraries attach importance to a borrower's record which will show what books are charged out to a reader. The purpose of the reading study determines the nature of the data which the investigator needs to assemble.

7.3 Single Record Charging System

Some libraries employ systems which combine the two records on a single card and provide a simple, quick way to check the back or class file and withdraw charges for overdue books. A coloured card can be maintained for a single record. A temporary call card made out by the circulation assistant at the loan desk. Another system is used based on a call card especially desired for a single charging record. The essential feature of the system is visible date tab which extends a quarter of an inch above the top of the charging card (3 × 5 inches). The same principle of a single record is followed in Punch and Machine System which is economical of sorting cards rapidly and accurately. Each card (3″ × 5″) has round holes punched adjacent to the edge of the card. The hole represent days in the week on which books are due. Overdues are withdrawn by removing the cards from the trays in groups and running a long sorting needle through the hole corresponding to the date being checked. Before the cards are returned to the file they are renotched to fall out one week later. The mechanical charging systems so successfully operated in public libraries.

The circulation department has also the responsibility of keeping statistics of library use and the types of materials used. If such figures are to serve a useful purpose in making comparison with the norm of other college libraries, they must be kept according to a standard form. The information called for includes: (1) the total number of volumes lent for home use, excluding reserve books; (2) the number of two-week loans; (3) the total circulation of reserve books; (4) the number of reserve books used in the building; and (5) the number of reserve books lent for overnight use.

7.4 Care of Book Collection

Since the library is concerned primarily with reading material much attention must be given to the physical care of the book collection. Requirements for the proper care of the collection include: (1) adequate space for the storage of books, with proper control of temperature and humidity; (2) space at the end of the shelves to allow for expansion without a constant shifting of volumes; (3) liberal use of book supports to hold books in place; (4) special shelving for quarto and folio books which require careful handling; and (5) provision for housing rare and finely printed material. As far as possible, the arrangement of books in the stacks should following the logical order of the classification system.

The care of the book collection involves more than provision for its physical arrangement. Reading material wear out, and it is necessary to make a continuous check on the collection to find worn volumes which need to be mended or rebound. The decision to rebind, replace, or withdraw a worn volume is based on answers to such questions as these: (1) Is the title available in a better edition? (2) Is there a later edition or more recent material in other books? (3) Is the old edition important for historical purposes, or does it contain something of value not in a more recent edition? (4) Is the title out of print and difficult to replace? (5) Are there several duplicate copies which are no longer in use lying idle on the shelves? This phase of circulation work requires a careful check of bibliographical aids, consultation with the faculty to determine the importance of the material and the best editions or translations for replacement, and close co-operation with the division of the library responsible for the preparation for binding.

7.5 Inter-Library Loan

Another aspect concerns inter-library loans. The circulation department is partly responsible for only that part of the work which has to do with sending out books to other libraries; and the reference department is responsible for borrowing books from other libraries. This procedure involves recording the books lent, the names of the librarians to whom they are sent, the date due, and sending notices to borrowing libraries that material is being sent — all types of routine which may be logically handled by the circulation department. The policy of the library in making requests for loans from other libraries should be consistent with its policy in lending to other libraries.

7.6 Reader's Privileges

Each library should consider providing facilities to: (1) seating space available for additional readers; (2) type of material which will be restricted for use within the building; and (3) regulations regarding registration, charging, and the return of books by these students.

Some libraries endeavour to develop special resources in some appropriate field of teaching or in printed matter related to a region or culture but a few, are repositories for books which one cannot find elsewhere. In so doing they place themselves under a certain obligation to make such material available to scholars everywhere. In most college libraries this privilege is accorded without question to visiting professors and scholars.

Regulations concerning the loan of books to campus or area readers are made to meet the needs of three groups of users: (1) undergraduates (2) graduates and (3) faculty or scholar (4) workers/labourers. Restrictions in use are justified only when they promote the interests of the majority or if the materials are especially rare.

7.7 Number and Length of Loans

Most of the libraries are facing problem in deciding what number should be number of books to be given on loan to the readers. With an adequate book collection, no restriction should be imposed but limit should be reasonable. A system of reservation of books should be established for the books which are more in demand and readers find it difficult to read such books. The following number is suggested:

College Library	–	Undergraduate	– 2
		Postgraduate	– 4
University Library	–	Research Scholar	– 6
		Faculty Members	– 10
School Library	–	Below 5th class	– 2
		Below 9th class	– 3
		Below 12th class	– 4
		12th class	– 5
Public Library	–	Regular Reader	– 5
		Casual Reader	– 2
Special Library	–	Research Scholars	– 15

The factors which determine the period of extended loans are:

(a) The teaching methods in particular institute.

(b) Type of reader and the nature of job.

(c) The size and quality of book collection.

(d) The speed and service capacity of the circulation section.

Faculty members are almost given special privileges because of research activities. All books issued to faculty members are renewed by hand or after physical checking during summer vacations keeping in view their demand.

Restricted Loans – It is the best policy not to issue any periodical but to allow their use in the campus of the library. Other restricted material is fine art and drawing books, illustrated books, college publications, reference books and reserve books. These books may be issued only in case there are duplicate copies and involves no high cost.

7.8 Overdue and Fines

It is the responsibility of the borrower to return books in time. Library send overdue notice if books are not returned in time. It is issued after 3-4 days of the expiry of overdue period and follow up.

It should be the effort of the library administration to minimise the fine or penalty if the number of defaulter is minimum. There are many system to levy library fine as under:

1. Fixed for a particular period:

   10 Paise per day upto return date

   10 Paise per day upto 15 days and then 20 Paise per day till return.

   25 Paise per day till date of return.
2. If fine is accumulated more than the cost of the book, the membership should be cancelled and the forwarding or recommending agency should be referred for necessary action at his level also.
3. Faculty members should not be charged any fine if 10% of the faculty members are defaulter. Fine may be imposed on faculty members if majority is habitual of not returning the book in time or at the end of the session.

In a library reserve books may be kept back of the main circulation desk because there is insufficient space or staff to handle them in a separate room. In the medium sized and large library the reserve books are kept in a special room or several rooms and are arranged either in a closed stack for circulation on rcquest or around the walls of the room on open shelves. The usual loan period is for two hours during the day and for overnight during the week, although most libraries now have a flexible policy of lending these books for various time limits. Books used only as suggested or collateral reading may be taken out for a longer than the two-hour period. Many courses find the three-day and one week loan a convenient one, and the system works well provided the fines are strict enough to insure prompt return of the books.

Since the reading of reserve books constitutes so large a proportion of the students' use of the library, their efficient administration is quite obviously a matter of great importance in teaching.

7.9 Circulation Services

The primary function of the circulation department of a library is to supply the library user the books, pamphlets, serials, maps, music, prints, microfilms, audio-visual and other material wanted on loan; maintain a record of all loans; keep a file of registered borrowers; provide machinery for the recall of overdue items and for reserving titles in demand; supervise the shelving of material in the stacks; arrange extension, inter-library, and public relations services; supply information for the replacement of lost items and make provision for readers to use materials in the library stacks.

7.9.1 *Registration of Borrowers*

Libraries require an established system of registering borrowers. The process of registration is determined with the size of the library, the nature and demands of the clientele and the safeguards of borrowing privileges. The main purposes of registration are (1) to know about borrowed and (2) the general characteristics of the borrowers as this involves some sort of agreement between the borrower and the library and responsibility on the part of the library to safeguard the property of the library and protect the rights of other borrowers. Registration files is maintained to provide information regarding the strength of the library and the statistics of circulation among different readers.

7.9.2 *Registration Procedure*

The registration procedure in libraries is fairly uniform. Commonly, every new reader is asked to complete a registration form, which is an agreement to observe the rules and regulations and guarantor's signature. This has all details of borrower.

A borrower's number is sometimes assigned to the application blank or registration form, and is also entered on the card given to the borrower. These cards may be filed numerically and form a numerical record of registration, though in some libraries the numerical file is kept in book form instead of on cards. Registration is usually for a definite period, say, for one to three years in many public libraries.

In Academic Libraries at the time of registration the student is to show an identification and received at the time of entry into the current academic period. The student is sometimes required to sign his name on the book card.

In some university libraries a visible file of registration is kept at the circulation desk. Each time a requisition slip (call slip) is presented the visible file is referred to: (a) to see whether the borrower is registered; (b) to check his signature; (c) to see if the borrower owes any fines.

A duplicate borrower card is generally issued for lost borrower's card and fee is charged for that.

7.10 Organization

The circulation department is organized according the size and scope of the library. Each type of library — public, college, university and special — has particular needs and the organization must reflect these needs.

The library has a central circulation desk which takes care of most circulation work. The academic library usually has supplementary service points including a periodical room, reserve desk, and departmental libraries. The large public library has its branches, deposit stations, and bookmobile service. In every library there should be a centralized organization to provide uniform loan and public services in all parts of the library system.

There should be a clear policy regarding service to users, hours of opening, borrowers' privileges, inter-library loan, fines, lost books. The head should be thoroughly conversant with the basic aims of the library as well as with the community or institution it serves.

Statistics reflect the success of the library. Statistics of borrowers recorded, of books issued and renewed or reserved, money received, etc. are recorded at the time of operations are performed.

Librarians must be in a position to know which materials are on loan, when they are due back in the library. The following statistics measure the work progress:

(a) *Book Record*: The record of a particular item.

(b) *Time Record*: ('Date due' file) shows when books are due back in the library. It shows which materials are overdue (*i.e.* for which the loan period has expired) so that the materials may be recalled for the use of other readers in demand.

(c) *Borrower's Record*: This record is sometimes used to indicate the number of books a borrower has out at one time.

7.11 Charging Systems

Photographic, mechanical, and marginal punched card charging systems have become widely used as charging system. The various mechanical systems which use primarily a transaction number for each withdrawal are most adaptable in the public library.

1. Ledger System accounts of books borrowed and kept under the borrower's name. The pages of the ledger were numbered and the page number was in effect, the registration number of the borrower. The details of the book (call number and issue date) were recorded under the borrower's name. When a book was returned the item was crossed through in the ledger.

2. Dummy System: It is used in small libraries (and board piece) dummy was used with the borrower's name on the spine. The dummy was maintained in an alphabetical file and was used as a substitute for the book on the shelves when the book was taken out for use. The call number and the date of issue were written on the dummy.

3. Card System: A book card which represented the book was used in most of the libraries. These cards were kept at the loan desk.

7.12 Circulation of Periodicals

Periodicals are not issued for home reading. They are issued for consultation in library campus.

REFERENCES

Beard, J.C. "Charging for Public Libraries." *IFLA.* 13, 4, 1987.

Dick, E. "What Happens to Library Circulated Books." *Lib. Qrly.* 18, 1948.

Douenes, R. "Who is Really Willing to Pay." *J. Acad. Lib.* 13, 1, 1988.

Foskett, A.C. "Shelf Classification or Else." *Lib. Jrl.* 95, 1970.

Lancaster, F.W. "If you want to Evaluate your library." London, *Lib. Asso.* 1988.

Rider, R. *Compact Book Storage.* New York, Hadham Press, 1949.

Sharma, C.K. *Dictionary of Lib. & Inf. Sc.* Delhi, Shree, 2002.

Sharma, C.K. *University Library: Management and Organization.* Delhi, Metropolitan, 1977.

Sohn, J. "Collection Development... ARL Libraries." *Lib. Res. & Tech. Services.* 31, 1987.

Wortman, W.A. "Collection Management." *Lib. Res. & Tech. Service.* 31, 4, 1987.

8

Acquisition Department

8.1 Introduction

After books are acquired, acquisition work begins. The first stage is the order work. Sometimes order work is included in book selection method where it is made on book selection cards. University libraries have a separate "Order Division" in Acquisition Department. Order division receives a great deal of new published books, reviews, catalogues, and other material which is also useful to the selectors. There are several points to be taken in account by the order division before issuing any order:

1. Whether funds are available for each faculty;
2. Whether the lists are approved by the proper authority for order;
3. Time taken in supply;
4. If the material ordered is not enough for the library.

The order department has also the responsibility to see that book funds are not overdrawn. In case a particular department lacks funds to meet essential needs, it should be assisted by mobilising the funds from the general department. Order department should be aware of the need and requirements of the various departments. When the books are received and checked with dealer's invoice, price and discount rates are verified for payment and sent to finance department. The book is marked in stock register. Published price is written in the accession register. The bill is verified and sent for necessary payment with the remark that 'the price charged, as cost of the book is according to the current published catalogue and checked with current price lists'.

Stock register number is written in the book on three places: on the back of the title page, on the secret page, and on the last page.

Accession register or the stock register is maintained in libraries. There are a number of columns which should be essentially filled in: serial number, name of the author, name of the title, edition, year of publication, publisher, format, size, classification number, price, source of purchasing, bill number and date of withdrawn, signature of withdrawing authority and remark.

In India one type of accession register is found almost in all the libraries. There are special supply agencies of library accessories who prepare registers of standard specifications and supply throughout India. It has been observed that the accession register is handled by many hands in the library which deface the accession register. The serial numbers written in various handwriting spoil the get up of the work. Serial numbers should be inscribed by numbering machine. The other alternative is to use the loose sheets and get the information typed on them. Later on they should be bound after 5000 books are entered in them.

Book selection is a part of Acquisition work. Book selection is processed by card system and list system.

Book selection cards are prepared at the time of receiving demands from the faculty and checked with catalogue and bibliographical tools. Every entry of order number, date of receipt, bill number, source author, title, the purpose and the nature of the book. Entries are made on the both sides. On the back of the card information concerned with order and acquisition procedure is noted, while on the front side of the card, the main entry of the book is made. The same card is transferred to the library catalogue after all acquisition process is complete, and used as shelf-list card mostly. The listing method is simple. The order is prepared in four copies. Two copies are sent to the supplier, one copy of finance department and one copy is kept in the library file. The suppliers supply the books and return one copy of list. This list is verified with office copy and the books. Many libraries maintain book selection cards.

After books are selected, they have to be secured by the library by a process commonly termed acquisitions. The former term is sometimes used to include book selection as well. In the small library the librarian will handle the order work in addition to his administrative and book selection duties. In the medium-sized library he may have an order librarian or at least a clerical assistant to help him. In the large library there will probably be an acquisition librarian with several professional and clerical assistants.

The acquisition department receives a great deal of information about books in announcements, reviews, catalogues, and in other forms frequently useful to the selector. A judicious selection of this material or notes based on the information contained in it should be routed to the book selection people. This point has already been mentioned in the discussion of participants in book selection.

The order department has in part the responsibility to see that books are ordered. If a department lags in sending in its orders, the cause may be plain faculty inertia, faulty ordering routine on the part of the library, or both. The order department should see that the channels for sending book orders are definite and satisfactory to the various departments. Proper forms or cards should be available for this purpose. Periodic statements of book balances should be sent to departments. The order department has also the responsibility to see that book funds are not overdrawn, or, if a particular department has not sufficient funds to meet essential needs, that funds are transferred from the general library fund or the material purchased from the general library fund.

8.2 Organization

All acquisitions are made in one of three ways: by purchase; by exchange; or by gift.

Purchase is, of course, the most important method, but the librarian who concentrates upon it to the exclusion of other types of acquisition will make a sad mistake. The problem of gifts, for example, is not something which can take care of itself. If the librarian is indifferent or cool toward gifts, he may, in the long run, discourage a certain amount of legitimate interest in the library.

The type of material exchanged is almost wholly confined to the results of research and the value for the library in exchange of publications is likely to hinge on the amount of the institution's participation in research. If the library has publications of its institution to offer and wishes to enter the field, the way of exchange has been pretty well marked out in the extensive practice of many university libraries.

Except for the "selection" of certain kinds of gifts, organization for acquisition work is essentially the same for gifts, exchanges, and purchases. The process should be straight and undeviating from selection through checking and ordering till the book and all the pertinent information about its arrival is safely in the hands of the cataloguer.

The major duties involved are:

1. Personal examination of all requests for orders to determine whether the library already has them, and where and how to order them.
2. Supervision and handling of all orders whether acquired by purchase, gift, or exchange.
3. Making recommendations to the librarian and members regarding desirable purchases based on first-hand acquaintance with the strength and weakness of the collection. This calls for a systematic plan of continuous co-operation among the various departments of the library.
4. Keeping accurate records of book fund accounts in order to avoid purchases in excess of departmental allocations, to show where departments are lagging in book orders and need to be stimulated.

8.2.1 *Order Routine*

Library has developed a "two-card" order system, in which one card is finally used in the shelf-list. Another system that has much to be said for it is that of multiple order slips. With a single typing of the order form, a number of carbon copies are made. Five such copies might be distributed this way: (1) the first copy to the dealer as the order; (2) the second and third copies to the outstanding order file; and (3) the fourth (a stiff card) to the main catalogue as a temporary author or main entry card. When books are received and checked, the third copy of the card may be forwarded to the catalogue department to be used as a work-slip. This method, particularly when the mechanical process is simplified with a billing typewriter, saves much paper work.

An adequate routine will proceed something like this:

1. A request or order card arrives with as many of the bibliographical details on it as the person asking for the book can be persuaded to supply, together with his name, the name of the department, and perhaps the initials of the head of the department who approves the order.
2. The card goes to the librarian who approves the order or indicates his reasons why he thinks the book or books should not be ordered.
3. The card is checked with trade bibliographies, and the bibliographical facts corrected or supplemented as necessary.
4. The card is checked with the library catalogue, the books-on-order file, and the books-in-process file to make certain that the book wanted is not already present, about to arrive, or in process of being catalogued and made ready for the shelves.
5. The bibliographical facts are set down in an order letter along with the facts about other books to be ordered. The date of order and name of the book dealer are entered on the card, and the card is filed alphabetically by author in a file of books-on-order.
6. The book arrives and is checked with the bill. Date and net price are entered on the order card. The price is charged against the appropriate book fund or department allotment.
7. The book is sent forward for preparation for the shelves.

8.2.2 *Order Procedures*

Order procedure should be based on three factors:

1. Effective and proper policy,

2. Adequate systems,
3. Keeping in view the objectives of the library.

Before starting order-work the librarian should decide:

1. Which order forms are to be used? What will be the proforma?
2. Whether easily available or easily preferable.
3. Whether mechanical or manual application.

8.2.3 *Ordering*

Ordering procedure will be as follows:

(a) Completing order cards with full details of supplier. If order-forms are used, these should have full details of the material to be purchased and the supplier,

(b) Preparing order-cards or forms in three copies,

(c) Signed by proper authority,

(d) Dispatching the orders by effective or speedy mail,

(e) Filing order cards or forms according to the status of the material — type of material, subject-wise, department-wise.

(f) One copy to be sent to concerned section, department, scientist or reader.

8.2.4 *Checking of Order-cards*

Checking work includes:

1. Checking of such order cards which are left unchecked,
2. Order-cards should be checked with catalogue entries,
3. Checking order-cards against ready-to-order files,
4. Order-cards are prepared as per details of bibliographical details.

Acquisition department is the first department in work-proceeding rating. It is an important department which:

(a) Obtains the material,

(b) Prepares the material for use.

This department has no relation with readers. It is behind the screen. Libraries with large annual accessions are likely to be organized into subscriptions on the basis of:

1. Form of material — Macro-documents or Micro-documents.
2. Method of acquisition — File system or order card system.

In big libraries both the types of materials are processed in separate and concerned departments *e.g.* Macro-document in Acquisition Department and Micro-documents in periodical or reference departments. But it depends on the librarian to decide.

8.3 Serial

Big libraries like university libraries or special libraries maintain separate Acquisition department. It is generally housed near reference department and circulation department. Serials can be divided in two division of material — Periodicals and other serials.

8.3.1 *Periodicals*

Periodicals are treated on separately in Periodical departments. Periodicals are received in this department and processed. Periodicals are treated as under:

(a) Receiving of periodicals,

(b) Recording of periodicals,

(c) Distributing periodicals,

(d) Transfer of periodicals to Binding department,

(e) Receiving back the periodicals from binding department,

(f) Arranging the periodicals.

Periodical department deals with current periodicals *e.g.*

(a) Selection of new periodicals on the basis of demand of the faculty members and specialists.

(b) Ordering of periodicals.

(c) Accessioning of periodicals.

(d) Treatment of periodicals

(e) Deciding the vendors/dealers of current periodicals.

(f) Provision of funds for periodicals.

In fact in large libraries specimen copies are obtained from the publishers and sent to the subject experts for their opinion. After receiving the opinion the order is issued and periodical is obtained. The periodical after obtaining the opinion of the experts is put before the library committee for approval. In university libraries, librarian himself takes final decision.

8.3.2 *Subscription Methods*

Whatever periodicals are selected they are processed as under:

(a) Method is decided first,

(b) Selection of agent or dealer. It should be —

  (i) an agent of repute,

  (ii) an established agent,

  (iii) agent under approach

(c) Direct method is also adopted. In this method periodicals are ordered to the publishers directly, but it requires —

  (i) Separate staff for acquisition work.

  (ii) A good amount for sundry expenses, *i.e.* stationery, postage etc.

  (iii) Maintaining the bibliographies in periodical department for latest informations.

  (iv) Contact with Reserve Bank of India or State Bank of India to have knowledge of current foreign currency rates or follow Good Office Committee information circulated from time to time on change in foreign currency rates/conversion rates.

Indirect method means subscribing journals through subscription agencies. It is better for Indian libraries to assign the responsibility to an experienced dealer or agent who has a sound financial position and foreign exchange permits. Libraries decide terms and conditions with subscription agencies beforehand on —

(a) Rate of interest,

(b) Discount rates, if available,

(c) Handling charges, if it is a publisher's condition,
(d) Supply through ordinary post, surface mail or Air mail,
(e) Replacement of missing issues,
(f) Indemnity bond to be executed.

Other Serials

There are other serials other than periodicals like reference books, newspapers etc. Reference books are treated like general books and accessioned in Acquisition section and transferred to reference department and periodical department.

Newspapers are treated in periodical department and recorded in separate newspaper registers.

8.3.3 *Various Systems Applied for Maintaining Records of Periodicals*

8.3.3.1 *Ledger System*: While periodicals are received in library, they are entered in a periodical Ledger Register. It is maintained in an alphabetical or numerical manner. One page is devoted to each periodical. An index is given in the starting of the ledger register maintaining the page number of each periodical recorded. Each page has following details:

(a) Name of the library. Generally large libraries print their name on each page of the ledger register,
(b) Name of the periodical,
(c) Publication frequency,
(d) Full address of the publisher,
(e) Full detail of the agency or supplier,
(f) Subscription amount in original currency,
(g) Subscription amount paid in local currency.

Sample

Name of the Library

Title__________________ Frequency________________

Publisher________________ Agency/Supplier_____________

Subscription Amount: Foreign Currency________________

Local Currency__________________

Year Vol.	Jan	Feb	Mar	Apl	May	Jun	Jul	Aug	Sep	Oct	Nov	Dec	Bill No. & Date	Remarks
1991 V.37														
1992 V.38														
1993 V.39														
1994 V.40														
1995 V.41														
1996 V.42														
1997 V.43														
1998 V.44														

8.3.3.2 *Register System*: This is another system applied in medium or small libraries. In this system record is maintained on the basis of frequency — *Monthly, Quarterly, Bio-Annual and Annual.*

Sample

Name of the Library

Frequency __________________ Quarterly________________

Supplier __________________ Publisher________________

Sl. No.	Title	Vol.	Period				Bill No. & Date	Remarks
			I	II	III	IV		
1.	A							
2.	B							
3.	C							
4.	D							
5.	E							
6.	F							

For periodicals supplied daily, weekly or fortnightly, the following register is used. One page is allotted for each such periodicals.

Sample

Name of the Library

Title________________ Frequency____________

Publisher______________ Supplier ____________

Year ________________ Subscription____________

Sl. No.	Month	Days							Remarks
		1	2	3	4	5	6...	31	
1.	Jan								
2.	Feb								
3.	Mar								
4.	Apr								
5.	May								
6.	Jun								
7.	Jul								
8.	Aug								
9.	Sep								
10.	Oct								
11.	Nov								
12.	Dec								

8.3.3.3 *Three Card System (S.R. Ranganathan)*: It is a good system and superior to all other system. It is initiated by Dr. S.R. Ranganathan. In order to keep an automatic check as to whether subscribed periodicals or magazines are being received regularly so that reminders may be sent in time. Dr. Ranganathan recommended "three card system". This system require less staff. It was first practiced in Madras University.

All the three cards are of size of 5″ × 3″ are:

1. Register Card
2. Check Card
3. Classified Index Card

1. **Register card:** This card is maintained as main card to record regular receipt of the periodical. It has full detail of the periodical and the availability of the periodical in the library.

Sample

Name of Library

Title	Payment	
Vendor	Vol. Or year	Voucher No. & Date
Publisher	Annual Subscription	

Class No.	Period in weeks/ Grace weeks	Order No. and date

Vol. & No.	Date of Pub.	Date of Receipt	Vol. & No.	Date of Pub.	Date of Receipt

2. **Check card:** It is card to help checking whether periodicals are received regularly and which periodical is missing.

Sample

Heading ______________________ Period ______________________

Grace weeks

vol. of issue	Due week	Week of return	Libn.'s sign	vol. of issue	Due week	Week of return	Libn.'s initials	vol. of issue	Due week	Week of return	Libn.'s initials

3. **Classified index card:** It provides additional information to the reader regarding the periodicals on a particular subject received in the library, including holdings like suppliments and cumulative indexes. These cards are arranged in a classified sequence.

Sample

Class No	Annual Subscription	Period in Weeks
Title Vendor Publisher Vol. Available Indexes etc. Supplements etc		

The numbering of the guide cards and the shifting of the check cards depend upon the frequency of the periodical. If publication is weekly, monthly, quarterly etc. the numbering will be —

First figure devotes the month number

Second figure denotes the week number

If publication is a weekly, the next due date = 2-3

If publication is a fortnightly, the next due date = 2-5

If publication is a monthly, the next due date = 3-3

If publication is a quarterly, the next due date = 5-3

When a reminder send for an issue of periodical not received the issue number is mentioned in the appropriate column of the check card, which is then shifted to its next due week.

Generally the following grace days are allowed for reminders —

For weeklies - one week

For fortnightly - one fortnight

For monthly - one month

When all issues of periodicals are received, loose issues are collected and arranged and sent to Binding section or the binder for binding. Binding will be as under:

(a) One binding for one volume.

(b) If it is annual volume, more than one volume but not more than two (2 years) should have one binding.

Other System

8.3.3.4 *Kardex System*: There are three types of cardex —

1. Horizontal card index
2. The Robot Kardex
3. Kardex

These kardex are used for recording the periodicals. The horizontal card index lie flat. Each card projects a little in front of the one following so that the cards lie in shallow drawers of the cards lying flat show the titles of the periodicals at a glance. The detailed entries are entered on the card in ordinary handwriting. It is a good system and safe. There are two drawbacks that first the tray is pulled out to its fullest extend and the required card is to be raised to the vertical position. Insertion of new cards is also seems inconvenient.

The Robot kardex system is improved form of horizontal card index. It was invented by M/s. Remington Rand of U.S.A. This form invented 'Robot kardex'. It is visible record for periodicals. In this system the Robot kardex unit contains sixty slides in two banks of thirty slides each, which moves up and down on a runner. While selecting the desired slide on the indexed keys and pressing down on the left and right end of the key the desired slide comes out on the desk extension rack. The size of cabinet is approximately 26" wide, 64" high, and 54" deep of depth consists of a desk extension at which the operator sits. It is about 32" high. The system requires an area of 13-4 sq.ft. and holds 4020 cards of 5" × 8" which are visible indexed.

The other system is 'kardex'. It is also invented by Ramington Rand of India Ltd. It is made of steel. The cabinet is approx. 10½" broad by 24" deep by 20½" high. One unit contains 7 trays containing 504 card holders with sliding dust cover and locking device. Bottom and top cards are available for replacement. A bottom card is prepared for each periodical and title. These are typed and written on the lower portion of the said card. The other columns in the card are:

(a) Library has
(b) Library lacks
(c) In binary
(d) Nature of binding

This card serves the purpose of keeping record of payments made to dealers and provides information regarding the follow up work connected with the receipt of the period.

Bottom Card

Name of Library

Year	Vol.	Jan	Feb	Mar	Apl	May	Jun	Jul	Aug	Sep	Oct	Nov	Dec	Index

Frequency________________ Current Vol. ____________

Department ________________ Vol. Per year ____________

Subscription expires on ________________________

Title ____________________________________

Library has ________________ Library lacks ____________

Top Card

Name of Library

Title ______________________ Call No. ____________________

Publisher__________________

Year	Vol.	Jan	Feb	Mar	Apl	May	Jun	Jul	Aug	Sep	Oct	Nov	Dec	Index

8.4 Acquisition Work

While the average number of books added annually in a library it is apparent that the larger enrolments are adding many more books than those with small enrolments. It may be pointed out that the number of new books being published each year is constant and therefore the small library presumably should be adding as many of these titles. The nature and character of the work done in organization has a direct bearing on the selection and acquisition of books. The gross size of the book collection is not a matter of real significance in measuring the adequacy of the library or in determining its book selection and acquisition policy.

It has not mattered whether the libraries are large or small. It also does not matter whether it is any particular decade in which special amount is increased. In fact the growth is real problem. There has been a direct correlation between the educational effectiveness, research-oriented courses, increase in literacy. Correlation is so close and so consistent that it is obvious that any slackness in the growth of library will slip the institution. However, there is no single evaluation which may be perfect and adequate. But combination of several may be expected to produce a picture of the adequacy of its book collection. The most common measure is to check the library's holdings against standard list of recommended books. Limitations lie in the varying nature of the library's book needs.

8.4.1 *Funds Available*

Other factors effecting book collection are the physical nature of library building, the nature and activities of reader's interest, the specific conditions, and the precedents existing in the library. All vary according to nature and size of library. In fact funds are generated and not always the same. The problem of funds might well be approached in another way. The administration will appropriate a certain year sum for buying books. If the funds are not sufficient the librarian should speak to the authorities and also suggest some measures to improve the funds. The funds should be sufficient to meet:

(a) The minimum needs of the library collection.

(b) The funds should be channelised to make justice with all type of readers and the courses, or educational programme.

(c) There are frequently small special funds which occurs to the library.

First, the librarian must see that enough funds are provided to permit purchase of an adequate number of good and useful books for library shelves. Second, he will ask operation of the faculty in the book selection process and "will make sure that the individual members are capable of furnishing this co-operation". Third, the librarian should be a capable person. The librarian should be aware that they, too, ought to suggest books for purchase. Certainly the library should be at pains to call to his attention and provide, upon his suggestion, books dealing with the newer developments in higher education and personnel administration.

Librarian should have close co-operation with faculty members and the readers. But it is generally seen that the relations among both are not so close as should be. They should discuss readers' problems, their demand and decide to select best books out of vast publication of books. Both the parties should have good knowledge of bibliographic activities. No doubt the book selection resulted to Laissez-faire philosophy. If the book selector or the faculty member has good knowledge of this field and capable to handle and guide the readers/students, he should be left free to book selection. He should keep in contact with all bibliographical sources and latest publications. There are many sources:

1. Publishers Catalogue,
2. Readers demand,

3. Bibliographical tools,
4. Review journals,
5. Librarian's personal contact.

In fact there is need for more specific information that will reveal more exactly the extent to which faculty members should be expected to make selection, and need for a determination of the types of material for which they are best equipped and trained to choose:

1. Abstracting and scholarly or technical journals containing reviews are usually regarded as reliable sources of information about books. The library must provide the most important of these journals and make them available to faculty in a way that will encourage their use as book selection tools.
2. Bibliographies in books and journals and even footnote bibliographical citations are commonly used as sources of information about books. A listing of the more important journals in subject fields which contain frequent bibliographies and book summaries would prove useful. The library has the means for finding such information through the Bibliographic index.
3. Most faculty members and academicians use subject bibliographies at least occasionally in selecting books for purchase. More use of these important tools could be made.

Good book selection not only involves a carefully formulated policy of book selection and faculty co-operation, but some definite organization. The following suggestions would seem to apply:

1. A department may properly order material which is immediately useful to it even though this material may be intended primarily as a contribution to some allied field.
2. In some departments a head appoints a member of the staff to be responsible for receiving all recommendations for purchase by that department.

The library committee also has an important stake in book selection. It must not, however, be allowed to take over any of the administrative functions which legitimately belong to the librarian. The library committee is not important in the job of selection. It can be particularly useful if it is representative of the whole faculty, not simply of particular departments, and if it can become on occasion a point of close liaison between the librarian and the faculty as a group.

8.4.2 *Librarian*

In order to administer the selection of books effectively, the librarian must have a thorough knowledge of the purposes of the organization and of the integration of the library with instruction. He must be a person of broad knowledge, trained in the methods of evaluating books, and must be willing to spend the time and effort to keep informed on the current output. He must be able to see the library collection as a whole and to assess its strengths and weaknesses.

Some of the essential duties of the librarian in book selection are to:

1. Direct the total process of book selection along sound lines. He should plan a long-range programme for the development of the collection with reference to what to select and where and how to select most economically and efficiently.
2. Afford the administrative officers a clear understanding of the significance of this programme in attaining the objectives and of the funds needed to support it.
3. Call upon the library committee for help in allocating book funds in such a way as to inspire interest and confidence.
4. Administer the book fund in such a way as not only to secure full faculty co-operation but at the same time to provide a sufficient general fund to develop the reference collections, the periodical files, and the books for general reading and to take care of expensive sets which no one department can afford to purchase from its allocation.
5. Study regularly bibliographies, book-reviewing media, catalogues, and other book selection aids which may suggest desirable purchases or information which

should be called to the attention of the faculty and members.

There the holdings of the library, subject to the special interests of faculty members, had developed in depth but not in breadth. The library staff committee, pooling staff knowledge, has managed to fill in many gaps and round out the collection. It should be one of the duties of the resourceful chief librarian to tap and energize this knowledge. The chief librarian, take responsibility for the book selection process is both an administrative and educational responsibility. In addition to handling the purchase of books, he exercises control over the programme of their selection. This responsibility is in line with the general administrative principle that in any organization there must be a central controlling factor to guide and co-ordinate activities. The librarian must select many books himself, but the ability to secure the full co-operation of everyone on the competent campus.

8.4.3 *Selection Policy*

There seems to be a good deal of haphazardness about the way in which most libraries book collections are built up. The faculty initiate most of the orders in the special fields of their several departments of instruction.

The library wants first, of course, to get the books needed for instruction and for direct study and investigation and eradication of literacy. Book çollection needs some standards:

1. Standard books should be selected.
2. Book should be of reference nature also.
3. Book collection should contain standard reference books useful for specific field.
4. An adequate stock of books for study courses and leisure readings.
5. The library should receive, bind and preserve accessibly a selected number of general periodicals.

There is a tendency to buy current books to an extent and leave little money for filling gaps of reference books. There should be a budget plan each year for building up the journal files and filling in gaps in the book collection in one major field.

This is a ticklish problem how much and which rare books should be purchased. Such books have a narrow but valid aesthetic and historical value which cannot be denied. Rare books should be purchased in university and reference libraries, but discouraged in small and college libraries.

There should be no rigid policy of buying fiction. One library buys no fiction until it is two years old on the theory that even if the books are permanently valuable they are worn out in the first rush of their popularity, and that selection of that which is tested can best be made at the end of two years. A middle ground on this question is taken by the libraries, probably the majority, which apportion a definite, limited amount of money each year for the purchase of such material. A frequent and careful discarding of unneeded duplicates after the demand for the title no longer exists is necessary to keep the stack shelves from being cluttered up with dead wood.

It is exceedingly difficult to draw the line which hypothetically divides material for readers from material for advanced research. Certain cases are obvious. The purchase of research material solely for individual faculty use should be subordinated to the adequate fulfilment of the primary book needs. Such material is no doubt useful for research libraries but it can also obtain under Inter-library loan from other libraries including National Library.

8.4.4 *Procurement*

Libraries obtain most of their acquisitions through several, if not all, of the following sources: publishers, book jobbers and dealers, local booksellers, second-hand booksellers, subscription agents. For the individual library, one or two of these agents will seem more important than the others, but each one has special advantages for certain kinds of purchases.

It is frequently true that a publisher will give greater discounts on book purchases than other agents, but any supposed advantage in such discounts will quickly be set down as a financial illusion when an examination is made of the increased paper work necessary to maintain it on any more than a nominal scale. Particularly in small libraries, whose minimum staffs continually struggle for time to do the more important educational jobs demanded of them, the ordering of books from many agencies is an uneconomic use of time, effort, and money.

The best source of books available to the library is the book jobber or dealer. He is able to give a substantial discount on bulk orders. He is familiar with library procedures and with library needs. If he handles the bulk of the library orders, he may also be prepared to handle smaller items on which he makes no profit, and special purchases like continuations and even out-of-print books.

The selection of a good supplier may involve these considerations:

1. Personal acquaintance with his organization or knowledge of his service from libraries acquainted with it.
2. *Discounts*: These will depend on (a) the volume of library business; (b) type of materials bought; (c) the ability of the dealer to supply some books in good condition; (d) the efficiency with which library orders are prepared and sent to the dealer.
3. *Service*: The book sellers service to a library can be measured by the size of his stock, promptness and care with delivery, transportation arrangements, and method and ease of adjustments. One very important point to consider also is the "follow-up" — the accuracy and the promptness with which a dealer reports back on "shorts" on out-of-print and out-of-stock items.
4. Purchasing from a local bookseller has usually proved unsatisfactory. His experience and the size of his stock seldom allow him to meet library needs, and the greater part of the library's requirements he will not have on hand.
5. Most out-of-print books are old. Those not second-hand will usually be denoted as "mint condition", "dust wrappers", or "as new" — notations which indicate top physical condition but which will not greatly mark them off from sound second-hand copies unless the books are rare.

6. The out-of-print dealer usually comes next in importance after the booksellers. The librarian has been advised to work regularly through one to two dealers as a sound practice. If more than two dealers are used, it involves excessive office and clerical work to be fair with the dealers by keeping them posted on items supplied, it may create an artificial rise in prices for particular books, and it may discourage the out-of-print dealer in his efforts. Advantages of this system will be the stimulus of competition and greater speed in securing out-of-print items.
7. Subscription agents are representatives who take orders for material and sometimes ask payment in advance of delivery. These representatives visit libraries for the purpose of selling in advance expensive reference sets not ordinarily sold through the regular trade channels. If the agent directly represents a reputable publisher, the chances are that his product is a good one and worthy of careful consideration. Subscriptions agents' offers should be: (1) checked with the Subscription books bulletin; (2) ordered, if possible, an approval for inspection; and (3) purchased only when they fill a particular need.

8.4.5 *Serials*

A serial has been defined as any publication, whether issued at regular or irregular intervals, with some scheme for consecutive numbering, and intended to be continued indefinitely. By definition, then, serials include annuals, monographs, and government publications in series, periodicals, and continuations such as almanacs, year books, proceedings, and transactions. In the large library the most important body of serials are the journals and government publications.

Serials are particularly important for the advanced studies preparing term papers who may need thesis source materials. The use of scholarly journals in the humanities and social sciences is equally important to the faculty. The reading of the results of recent scholarship in these fields is as necessary for instruction and research as is familiarity with recent advances in chemistry or physics.

In an effort to attain objectivity in the selection of periodicals at least three statistical methods have been used. In one of these the opinions of a varied group of experts was statistically summarized for a considerable list of periodicals. The relative importance of journals in a particular field was determined by tabulation and summation of bibliographical references culled from key journals during a specified period. Since one or another of these methods has been applied to a number of other fields, the statistical plan of evaluation has obviously merited a certain amount of approval from experts. However, one real objection to the statistical method may obtain as applied to the selection of journals in the libraries.

The library is first obliged to meet the primary needs of the many rather than the unusual needs of a few. Even large libraries find it difficult to secure and maintain files for all their needs. In consequence the idea of co-operation has received more and more favourable attention in determining the acquisition of journals in college libraries.

A considerable diversity of practice in the handling of serials from the point of selection to the point of use is noticeable in academic library practice.

The case for the centralized serials department in which all work relating to serials is carried on would seem to have real advantages where the staff is sufficiently large, where the physical condition are right. It would not seem that the separate serials department could be fully recommended when by that is meant the placing of all ordering, checking in, cataloguing, and reference work with serials under a separately organized part of the library staff. Many libraries would prefer to keep reference service under the direction of the reference department. It is not possible to classify readers. When a reader comes to the library no one on earth can tell in advance whether the information he wants is to be found in serials, books, or in other types of materials. It is likely, moreover, that the concentration of financial accounts in one department is more efficient and desirable. And it is certainly true that for many libraries, the cost for additional staff would be prohibitive. The most practicable working arrangement would seem to be a combination of methods working through the regularly established departments of the libraries. Under such a plan the organization of work might be laid out in this manner:

1. The acquisition of all serial matter would be handled in a separate division of the order department. If there are no divisions in the department, the records and routines for handling serials would still be kept separate and distinct by the person responsible for ordering.
2. The serials record in the order department should be a complete file of all information necessary for the acquisition, treatment, and use of serials. This record will be for the use of the library staff, and essentially for the serials division; since its detail may make it unintelligible to readers, it may be inconveniently placed for their inspection, and they may not be inclined to seek it out.
3. There should also be kept a "visible index" of periodicals for convenience in handling reference questions.
4. The person in-charge of this work might also be responsible for the binding of serials. The serials record is invaluable for this purpose even though it may not always be practical to combine the binding record with it.

There are a number of good magazine subscription agencies, and far better service will be secured if orders for journals are placed with one of them than with publishers or with a local agency. The advantages of the national magazine agency are several:

1. Billing is done at one time, annually.
2. A reliable agency will notify a library of changes in a magazine's status and follow up missing numbers or errors in mailing.
3. Continuity in receipt of issues is better assured.
4. Cost adjustments are more easily made.
5. Discount will be greater since the local agent will himself be dealing through a national agent.
6. Routine work of the library is greatly reduced.

There are a number of other general rules to follow in placing subscriptions. For one thing, the library should avoid the immediate closing or beginning of the calendar year in placing its subscriptions since the dealer is swamped at that time with gift and other individual orders.

8.4.5.1 *Exchange*: The value of exchange of periodical files has always been recognized more widely than that of other material. There are agencies providing this service but libraries for the most part have operated independently, issuing "want" and "exchange" lists on the basis of first come, first served.

8.4.5.2 *Binding*: Periodicals are the backbone of a library's reference materials. They represent a substantial and continuing investment which must be safeguarded by sufficient funds for binding and rebinding. Such binding should be done regularly. To postpone binding from year to year, to risk the possible loss of unbound numbers of journals, and to allow expensive books and journals to depreciate through neglect of binding or a poor quality of binding is unsound library administration and false economy. There are, however, some materials which may be bound in a cheaper binding without sacrificing the investment of the library and with considerable benefit to users of the library. Lettering is omitted and must be done by the library. These economies permit a much lower charge for binding. The amount of material which can be bound in this manner is definitely limited and should be carefully scrutinized by the librarian before it is sent to the binder.

Magazines which are indexed in the general indexes and whose back files are frequently called for should be bound since a good quality of binding gives them durability and maximizes the chances of keeping them intact. A close working relationship between the library and the bindery will pay dividends in good binding. In preparation well before the expected date of binding, the file of a volume of magazine should be examined for missing numbers, those numbers should be ordered from the publisher or magazine agent, and title pages and indexes for such magazines as furnish them should also be asked for.

8.4.6 *Government Publications*

Librarian have frequently noted the importance of "documents" for reference work; useful types, for example, are census material and the reports of government investigation and research, and of course, those publications giving facts about the personnel and structure of the government itself. There can be no doubt of the general usefulness of government publications not of the variety of purposes which they can serve.

The handling of these publications, however, is complicated by at least two important factors. One difficulty is inherent in the mass and variety of the government output. There are indexes and bibliographical apparatus designed to unlock this material for general use; but such has been the helter-skelter expansion of "ephemeral" material in near-print form that there has been no available index both inclusive and up-to-date.

8.4.6.1 *Selection*: Nearly all depository libraries are "partial" depositories. By prearrangement they already receive certain publications, and for them selection cannot be said to be the continuing problem which it is for the non-depository. The librarian in the non-depository library will have no question about the need for such standard reference works as the statistical abstract etc. It is impossible to make out a list of government publications required in every library, but it can be said that identification of indispensables for a particular library is much simpler than the problem of selection which begins where the indispensables leave off.

Primary tools of selection will be the file of the Monthly catalogue for older publications, and for current material the latest issue of the Monthly catalogue; Selection government publications, now published semi-monthly; selected listings in the Publisher's weekly. Other leads to current publications may be the announcements of government reports in newspapers and the selected lists published frequently in the official journals in special fields.

8.4.6.2 *Ordering*: Government publications can be acquired by request from the representative of the congressional district in which the library is located by purchase from the Superintendent of Government publications, by request from.

In any case some of the library's most substantial reference works and continuations must be purchased. Furthermore, perhaps because sales prices are at cost and congressional distribution has sometimes been wasteful, the trend in government opinion has been toward placing more and more material under restrictions of purchase.

8.4.6.3 *Newspapers*: The small or medium-sized library will want to take one or more purely local newspapers, whether these turn out to be country weeklies or city dailies. And it will want to receive a number of weeklies of farm, labour, socialist, or other specialized interest. The smaller newspapers can frequently be obtained by gift. With these aspects in mind, even the smallest newspaper collection may take on a semblance of minimum adequacy.

The newspaper collection of the large library should be expanded well beyond such a minimum. It is likely to include a greater variety of regional domestic newspapers and a number of outstanding foreign newspapers to give breadth and as much national and international representativeness as possible. Another factor influencing selection may be the newspaper collections of other libraries in the vicinity. So costly and difficult is the maintenance of newspaper collections that usually the only adequate answer is regional collaboration. Especially is this true of preservation of back files.

A newspaper reading room is usually beyond the needs of a library. Current issues may be kept with current periodicals, either on shelves or fastened to sticks arranged on a rack. The space necessary for housing such files must not only be considerable but care should be taken that it is neither damp nor excessively dry. Most libraries will find the best accommodation in separate stacks or a particular section of the regular stacks, in which use can, if necessary, be restricted.

Binding is expensive, and as a method of preservation it is incomplete since it cannot protect newsprint from disintegration. If the library cannot afford to bind a newspaper but needs to keep a file of it, an inexpensive substitute method of outer protection is to wrap consecutive issues of a newspaper in heavy manila paper. Several librarians have called attention to the need for the indexing of local newspapers by libraries. A relatively quick and simple method is to index under specific headings, entering as many as fifty items on a single large card. Personnel and budget will usually not permit this "extra", either in a form so simplified or one more complete, but if they do and no public library in the vicinity can do the job the library may very well assume the responsibility for it.

8.4.7 *Pamphlets and Clippings*

New pamphlets are among the livest of materials dealing with current affairs and when they have grown old they can become the most curious, entertaining, and sometimes the most useful of source material for historical research. Librarians have seldom doubted the usefulness of pamphlets. The pamphlet may not seem as important material for the small library as for the public library. Nevertheless, the effort of the librarian to promote selection of pamphlets by members their use through publicity and displays should be worth-while. In some areas pamphlets are a leading form of material — in the labour field, for example, where much source material never appears in full in book form, and in vocational guidance where the conditions and interest may rapidly change.

8.4.8 *Rare Books*

What is a rare book? Roughly, it is any book printed before 1550, any English book printed before 1720, any book before 1800. The library which is able to build collections of all these types will be more rare than its own books. But nearly all libraries will have the opportunity to build collections in at least one or two of these fields. For example, the library which makes no effort to discover and build a collection of local imprints or of local historical material, provided no public or other library in the vicinity is making such as effort, is dull or impoverished indeed.

The rare book collection, if extensive, is probably best housed in a separate fireproof building with a full-time curator. A second choice is a separate room with a full or part time attendant and facilities for study. If this is not possible, locked rooms or screened-off sections of the stack are the best substitutes. There should be provision, of course, for qualified readers to work with such a collection. And there should be cases for the exhibition of such material either in the rare book room or elsewhere in the building. Rare books are certainly not to be treated in this respect like other library books. Adequate supervision should make unnecessary the usual book "preparation". A bookplate may well be used, but other necessary information can be pencilled in, and the shelf location can be indicated by a typed strip of paper which is slotted so that it may be slipped over the top edge of a back fly-leaf, and projects only slightly above the binding.

Some fear or distaste has been shown for the tone of propaganda which marks certain pamphlets. But this is nothing to cause fundamental difficulty.

A number of librarians have favoured treating pamphlets like books and giving them full cataloguing. It is unlikely, however, that the library will be able to cope with the flood of current material in this way except at the expense of other services, and it has been suggested that the time spent in cataloguing might better be put into publicizing a pamphlet file on the theory that a pamphlet file, catalogued or uncatalogued, that is well used is more to be desired than a catalogued file which is not used extensively.

A good method for handling such pamphlets will be simply to stamp them with library marks, place them on racks or shelves where they may easily be seen, and allow them to be borrowed. When their current use has passed, the library may wish to catalogue some and send others to vertical files, but many more will be discarded. A more frequent modern practice is the use of pamphlet boxes; pamphlets which are catalogued but have been left unbound can then be shelved advantageously alongside books on similar subjects without fear of physical damage.

Clippings have traditionally been included with pamphlets in a vertical file, clippings may not be so necessary as in public libraries. They will be useful, however, for the coverage of state and local affairs which are usually not indexed. Clippings may be mounted on cards or cardboard or put in envelopes and placed in the vertical file.

8.4.9 *Non-Book Material*

8.4.9.1 *Maps and Atlases*: Maps are a specialized kind of library material, there are perplexities in their selection, and there are both difficulty and expense in organizing and housing them. A map is defined as a graphic presentation of a portion of the surface of the earth on which we live, or even of the whole globe, on a plane surface, usually with a high degree of generalization and addition of data and some subject matter. An atlas is a collection of maps often made on various scales and containing various types. Principally because they represent a curved surface on a plane surface, maps are only approximations. Two maps representing exactly the same area and similar data may differ markedly according to the kind of projection. Hence for the cataloguer and the user of maps, the projection becomes one of the most important facts to be noted.

Other important uses for maps are for research, in drawing or preparing other maps on which various data are to be plotted, and for reference work in the library for the ascertaining or discovery of particular facts.

The selection of maps involves four factors: (a) area to be covered, (b) scale of map; (c) type of map, and (d) date.

Maps may be divided into three groups: large, medium, and small scale. Since it requires many sheets to cover an area on a large scale, the library is unlikely to be able to acquire this type except for the area immediately surrounding its geographical location. Small-scale maps are the kind usually found in atlases, aiming at representing on a single sheet an entire country or a continent. Date will help to indicate changes or shifts in the basic information presented, and will be important also where an effort is made to acquire maps of an historical nature, the librarian is urged to select his date carefully and hew to the line since unplanned acquisition can be very expensive and inefficient.

A map collection frequently demands its own special accommodations in a separate room, or if it is not too large it can be incorporated in a general reference room. Equipment is specialized.

Cataloguing of maps is one of the more difficult of processes. Account must be taken of projection, because of the distortion inevitable with representing a curved surface on a plane surface; of the process of reproduction; of the authorship, frequently lost anonymity; of the title, sometimes given in two or more languages.

General Principles

1. To provide a definite position for each map in the map files in relation to very other map.
2. All such maps should bring together in the files which will be used frequently in association with another.
3. All peculiar informations regarding maps should be recorded on the catalogue card.
4. There should be uniformity in cataloguing.
5. Adequate system should be followed.
6. Heading should be similar to books and periodicals.

8.4.9.2 *Microfilm and Microcards*: Applications of micro-reproduction to library purposes have been changing and developing so fast that it is impossible to offer final opinions on their usefulness. More generalization and standardization of knowledge in this field is clearly needed.

Microcards are a form of micro-text on paper, and since paper is cheaper than film and is likely to spread fixed costs over a greater number of copies, microcards will in the end probably be less expensive. Furthermore, since microcards are simply standard-size library catalogue cards having on them a catalogue entry as well as the greatly reduced pages of the text, they bypass the problem of cataloguing, which still exists for microfilm. In many areas microcards seem preferable to microfilm.

The uses of microfilm and microcards are several. In fact no better gauge of their importance can be found than in the variety of their applications:

1. Microfilm has already penetrated the field of inter-library loan. Where articles from periodicals or chapters from books are asked for, a microfilm of the original can frequently be obtained for little or no more than

the expense of transporting the heavier materials, and the borrowing library or the individual for whom it borrows will frequently have the additional advantage of owning the film copy permanently.

Microcards will tend to reduce inter-library loan problems still further. For they should eventually make available for purchase by the library whole fields of fugitive and scarce materials which formerly were unobtainable or too expensive.

2. Microfilm, though photostat is preferable for short items, is economical, particularly for large blocks of material for which relatively few copies or reproductions are demanded. Microcards, for whatever materials they become available, should be even more inexpensive.
3. Microfilm is relatively permanent and can be used to reproduce impermanent materials like newspapers. As is well-known, modern newsprint distintegrates after a few years in spite of great care and the best protection.
4. Microfilm is tremendously saving of space. The saving of space by microcards will be even greater than that by microfilm, but it should be remembered that for the library, microcards will not so often displace bulky materials already owned as it will add new resources.

Organization: Microfilm can be shelved with books but it seems most advantageous to shelve it by itself. The latter method is mandatory where a humidifying cabinet is used; it simplifies classifying, and takes full advantage of the opportunity to save space.

Rolls of film are kept in small cardboard cartons and the cartons can be filed consecutively in cases large enough, if regular book shelving is used, to utilize the full depth of space originally intended for more bulky material. If film is shelved by itself, strips which are individually too short for a full reel can be spliced together, but in that case the sequence of items should be given on the carton.

Classification can be simply a film symbol followed by serial numbers given successively to the reels of microfilm as they are received, or where a serial run like a newspaper is currently being received, a variation of the scheme can be adopted. Cataloguing should be no more complicated than necessary, but should follow that for books with reasonable closeness. The author, title, date, and publisher should certainly be included, and specific reference to length and to the fact that the film is a copy should be incorporated.

8.4.9.3 *Music, Records and Recordings*: Indeed, so important has the record become that to speak of it, as is frequently done, as one of the "audio-visual aids" is something of a misnomer. For the musician the phonograph record may have become and may still remain only an important aid; but for the general reader, whose role must be largely limited to the appreciation of music, it has become, at least so far as the library is concerned, the primary material — with books and scores serving as aids.

Because of the importance of records, may now be included in it. If it is a lending collection, there may be needles and phonographs. Records available from commercial houses are by no means confined to music but include poetry recitations, dramatic episodes, and language and speech units.

The materials in a music collection — books, scores, sheet music, records, recordings, and special equipment — are important for teaching purposes in music, language, literature, speech, psychology, and other courses. Records can also be used in organized extra-curricular activities — for dances, for sound effects in college plays, and as background in the showing of silent motion pictures.

A record library may logically be built up around a core of the best known musical masterpieces. But to make certain the development of the library is even all along the way, the following outline might be followed:

I. *Music by great orchestras*

(a) Symphonies

(b) Concertos

(c) Ballot music

(d) Overtures

II. *Instrumental Music*

(a) Piano

(b) Violin

(c) Other instruments

III. *Music for Voice*

(a) Opera

(b) Choral music

(c) Song

IV. *Miscellaneous*

(a) Popular music

(b) Folk music

(c) Diction records

If the music collection is small, the number of phonograph records few or non-existent, and there is no phonograph, music could very well be shelved with other library materials in the main collection. Since this condition has become markedly less frequent among college libraries, the tendency has been toward having a separate music room or library. Such a music room should be large enough to make possible group listening. And since individual listening is quite as important, library tables should be equipped with turn tables and earphones. The music room will house not only music but other materials, particularly special or non-musical records, which naturally belong there; and it may prevent other demands for decentralization.

If the records are used chiefly within the music room they may be filed in horizontal drawers which drop to a vertical position when pulled out, in vertical files, on horizontal shelves, or vertically in heavy envelopes as they are in shops. If records are to be loaned frequently, they should be filed vertically in albums in the open cabinets, because albums offer the best protection for borrowing.

About the classifying and cataloguing of phonograph records there has been much different of opinion. At least four methods of classification have been suggested: (1) by form; (2) by company number; (3) by accession (used in closed stacks); and (4) by composer. These methods are recommended where records are kept in albums and are circulated a shelf-list will usually be necessary, and the catalogue will be called frequently into use. The catalogue will be particularly useful for the location of single records which may be grouped in "miscellaneous" albums. Where record jackets used in shelving records, they should be carefully labelled with the call number, composer, and title. The large music library will have its own catalogue and except for books on music, no duplicate entries would seem necessary for the main library catalogue.

8.4.9.4 *Visual Aids: Pictures, Slides, Filmstrips*: Many of the materials for learning, other than books, are considered today under the general term of audio-visual aids, and a few organizations have recently grouped all these aids together in a special department within the library.

Though libraries have not deliberately refused the handling of these materials, neither Academic nor other libraries have, for the most part, either promoted their full use or encouraged their growth in any orderly fashion. It is perhaps in the nature of accumulating practices to develop step by step. It is certainly true that while discussion of audio-visual aids in the library frequently groups them together, in actual practice they have more often been separated. The present-day library may have an excellent collection of one type of audio-visual material and little or nothing of other types.

Pictures: Picture collections may be acquired in many ways. It is possible to build a large useful collection from discarded books and magazines, from advertising material, rotogravure sections of newspapers, travel circulars, pamphlets and other sources.

The pictures in a small collection may be unmounted if filing space is limited. In that case they should be cut neatly with as wide margins as possible and placed in folders, or as one library has found feasible, in envelopes made from brown wrapping paper marked with appropriate subject headings. Filing cases should be of legal size of larger. Most libraries, however, prefer to mount their pictures on stiff mounting paper, oak tag, mat board, or binder's board. Pictures should be cut with a 1/8 to ¼ inch margin, and cutting for both picture and backing should be done with a Boston cutter. Top and side margins of the mat should be equal, the bottom margin somewhat larger.

In large libraries where the picture collection is extensive, material may be housed in boxes, but where the collection is to be examined by the borrower or user, it is preferable to use legal-size steel or wooden filing drawers or even better, filing cabinets made up of many compartments with a drop front for each tier.

There is no standardization in classification schemes, but most frequently perhaps the primary division of the collection is by subject such as architecture, sculpture, painting, and the various minor arts; under subject arrangement subdivisions are by period, country, and then alphabetically by city or artist. Another method is to divide material first into large culture cycles.

Slides: Standard slides (3¼" × 4") can be readily made by the individual, but libraries are likely to purchase most of theirs from recognized sources. Advantages of the slide are convenience and ease of projection, universality and adaptability, and the fact that it is the only projected visual aid which can be used successfully in a room not thoroughly darkened. Disadvantages are weight, tendency to breakage, and somewhat greater cost than such materials as the filmstrip. Slides will have to be kept separately in their own filing boxes or cabinets. It is important to have some system of arrangement by subject and to classify and catalogue them.

Filmstrips and Microslides: Housing of strips should be in small metal cartons as for microfilm, and sufficient humidity can be supplied if a bit of comphor gum wrapped in paper is placed in the container. It has been remarked that filmstrips in their form and use, are closer to motion pictures than to still pictures or slides, and this fact should be reflected in their cataloguing.

Filmstrips have two different forms: the single-frame slide, in which the width of the picture is across the film, necessitating that it be run through a projector vertically; and the double-frame slide, in which the width of the picture parallels the length of the film with the result that it must be run through a projector horizontally. Projectors should be purchased which will handle both types.

8.4.9.5 *Book Ordering System and Automation*: No doubt

computer order system is difficult but not impossible. It is the need of the day. It is expected to perform certain managerial functions in addition to clerical functions such as —

(a) Pre-order searching
(b) Creating purchasing order.

The system must usually respond to regular order, blanket orders and exchanges, etc. It must also be able to handle regular receipt, not receipt, out of point, documents with wrong billing, unwanted documents with right billing and so on.

Functions

The automated book ordering system performs the following functions:

1. Pre-order searching. It avoids duplication.
2. Creating purchase orders.
3. Providing information on orders outstanding.
4. Preparing vouchers to pay for the books.
5. Maintaining book fund accounts and printing book fund reports.

There is provision in system to issue reminders if supplier makes delay in supply. All account procedures are also handled by the system after receiving the books.

However, the system is effective in following activities:

(a) issuing reminder note,
(b) handling accounting procedures,
(c) preparing accession register as a by-product,
(d) bibliographical details may also be amended, if required by library staff to produce catalogue card,
(e) machine readable book cards can be punched automatically in 'order system'.

The computerized circulation system may generate reports from order file if —

1. All information or data are entered in the system regarding order number, author, title, country, language etc.

2. Claims or cancellation notices sent to supplier are entered,
3. Notices issued to supplier are entered.

Prerequisites: The following factors are kept considered before hand in computerized book-order system.

1. File maintained,
2. Data elements in the record of each file,
3. Record format,
4. Media of the file,
5. Mode of operation.

In one-line system files are access. The number of files depend on the size of the library. The following files may be maintained:

(a) Supplier file (SF)
(b) User file (UF)
(c) Search file (SEF)
(d) Order file (OF)
(e) Fund file (FF)
(f) Accession file (AF)
(g) Shelf file (SHF)

Data File

1. Supplier file (on tape or disk)	(i) Supplier Number
	(ii) Supplier name
	(iii) Address
	(iv) Telephone No.
	(v) Telex Number
	(vi) Cable
	(vii) Currency accepted
2. User file (On tape or disk)	(i) User Number
	(ii) User name
	(iii) Address
	(iv) Telephone Number

3. Search file (On tape or disk after preparing order file)	(i) User Number (ii) Supplier Number (iii) Author (iv) Title (v) Publisher (vi) Place of Publication (vii) Edition (viii) Volume Number (ix) Part Number (x) Estimated price (xi) ISBN Number
4. Order file (Tape or disk)	(i) Order Number (ii) As in search file
5. Accession file (Tape or disk)	(i) Date of accessioning (ii) Accession Number (iii) Data as in order file (iv) Cost of foreign currency (v) Cost of local currency (vi) Whether withdrawn (vii) Call Number (viii) Books by gift or not (ix) Books by exchange (x) Source of gift
6. Shelf test file (tape or disk)	Complete bibliographic data
7. Fund file	(i) Total fund (ii) Sources of funds (iii) Documents (iv) Amount withdrawn

Ravichandra Rao further describes that some systems have been developed in this file. Much to be done.

REFERENCES

Burse, G.V. "Co-operative Acquisition." *Lib. Trl.* 78, 1953

Downs, R.B. *Acquisition and Cataloguing of Books*. Ilhner's Stall, 1976.

Ford, Stephen. *The Acquisition of Library Material*. Chicago, Am. Lib. Asso., 1973.

Malathi, N. "Co-operative Acquisition." *Ind. Libn.* 23, 1968.

Manjunath, G.K. "Integrated Book Acquisition and Circulation System." *Procgs. of CDSIIIS User Groups*. Hyderabad, Feb. 1994.

Melcher, Daniel. *Acquisition*. Chicago, Am. Lib. Asso., 1971.

Ojha, S.R. *Punch Cards Control the Purchase of Publications*. Am. Lib. Sc. Doc. 24, 2, 1977.

Ragers, R.D. *University Library Admin*. New York, Wilson, 1971.

Sharma, C.K. *University Library: Management and Organization*. Delhi, Metropolitan, 1977.

9

STOCK-TAKING

9.1 Physical Verification

The holdings of a library may be checked at regular intervals to find out which items are missing. This task should be planned to ensure its competition with the least interruption to the library service. It is natural that some portion of library materials thrown open for public use are liable to be damaged and lost. But a stock-taking report is useful in determining whether the library's provisions for the protection of its materials are adequate.

It becomes difficult and inconvenient to do thorough physical verification of the holdings as it dislocates the regular library routine in diverting staff for stock-taking purposes. Effort should be made not to close the library or stop certain services for stock verification. Verification may be done section by section or class by class with the help of shelf-list without dislocating normal library routine.

Advantages

1. Stock verification discloses the position of the loss of books so that replacement may be made in case of essential books lost.

2. Misplaced books are restored to their proper places and this results in rectification of stock.

3. Stock verification provides adequate account of the percentage of inevitable loss.

4. It helps in planning the methods to provide adequate safeguards to check future losses.

5. Periodical stock-taking leads to the cleaning and dusting of books and thus prevents their deterioration.

6. It provides opportunities to weed out books no longer in use or long unused as well as very old editions of books.

7. It provides an opportunity to the members of the staff to acquaint themselves with the holdings of the library and thus help them to render better reference service.

Disadvantages

1. In case of periodicals, the working of a library is hindered for closure, or, its normal services are curtailed.

2. Stock-taking yields no tangible results while entailing at the same time wastage of money, man hours and materials.

3. The cost of stock-taking does not cover the cost of books misplaced and lost.

4. Books loaned out are called back much to the inconvenience of readers resulting in the break of loan services.

These reasons have covered the stock verification complete stock being abandoned by libraries and simpler methods of stock verification are being resorted to.

9.2 Stock-taking Methods

1. Shelf-list.
2. Accession Register.
3. Separate register with Accession Numbers.
4. Separate sheets containing Accession Numbers in a consecutive order.
5. Numerically counting the book on the shelves.
6. Computer machines.

9.2.1 *Stock-taking by Shelf-list*

Shelf-list cards arranged usually by classification numbers plus book numbers (call number) may be used for stock verification. The shelf-list cards may have special columns upto 20 years on its back side.

902 Sharma, C.K.

L26e

Modern Library System by C.K. Sharma

Agra, Y.K. Publishers, 1995

xi, 273p; 23cm

29782

1972	1973	1974	1975	1976	1977	1978	1979
1980	1981	1982	1983	1984	1985	1986	1987
1988	1989	1990	1991	1992	1993	1994	1995

A shelf-list drawer containing subject cards is taken to the shelves. One assistant speaks out the call number and Accession Numbers of each volume and another assistant checks the call number, tickmarks the relevant year column (in which stock-taking is done) and pushes forward the cards which have been checked. The cards bearing call numbers of books which are not found readily in the shelves are made to stand on their shorter edges. At the end of each day a list of these cards is made and checked with the out-on-loan records in the issue counter. The records in the bindery and the withdrawal register. From the list of cards representing books which are not traceable finally proper remarks are made in the Withdrawal Register. These shelf-list cards are then filed in a separate sequence known as Withdrawals sequence.

In some libraries the shelf-list has no space for columns. If such a shelf-list is used for stock-taking the cards for which books are found are pushed forward and those for which books are not traceable are made to stand on their shorter edges or marked with soft lead pencil. At the end of the day's work these cards are listed and checked with the records of the charging counter, bindery and withdrawal register. The standing cards are then put in their normal position.

The final list is again checked with shelves and with all arrangements like brcken order, 'parallel sequence' etc., and the entries of those books which are found there are crossed from the list.

Advantages

1. This system ensure speedy stock-taking and separate shelf-list trays may be used by different assistants to work simultaneously.

2. The shelf-list arrangement reflects the arrangement on the shelves checking is easier.

3. It helps the rectification of stock.

9.2.2 *Accession Register*

The Accession Register is taken to the shelves and one assistant calls the particulars of the books from the shelf along with the Accession Number, and another assistant ticks the relevant Accession Number in the Accessions Register. When all the books are checked, a list of books which could not be traced is prepared and such books are further searched from different records and a final list is prepared of the books not finally traced and reported to library committee.

This method is: (1) cumbersome; (2) time-consuming; (3) the ticks in the Accession Register disfigures and spoils the neat appearance; (4) books are arranged on the shelves by class number while the entries in the Accession Number are by serial numbers; (5) it takes a lot of time to search the Accession Number and verify the details of the book before ticking it; (6) the book traced is tick-marked in the Accession Register by a soft lead pencil; (7) this method is slow and is not suitable for a big library with a sizable collection.

9.2.3 *Separate Register*

In order to prevent disfigurement of the original Accession Register by ticking, and damage by constant handling, a separate stock-taking register with Accession Number and years is prepared.

Accessions No.	1972	1973	1974	1975	1976	Remarks
2456						
2457						
2458						
2459						
2460						

In this method two assistants carry out the stock-taking work. One assistant speaks out the Accession Number from the book and the other assistant ticks the relevant year column from the Accession Number spoken. At the end of stock-taking a list is prepared on separate sheets, untraceable books are traced as far as possible from the records in the charging counter (issue counter) and the Binding Section and also from the shelves of returned books and the items found are crossed out from the list. The remaining items are noted down on a separate paper with all relevant details and prices of the books, for the purpose of getting them written off with the sanction of the proper authority. The crossed items are tick-marked in the Stock-taking Register.

Advantages

This method saves the Accession Register from disfigurement and damage. But there are chances of speaking out wrong Accession Number or crossing out wrong numbers still remains.

The preparation of separate Register when the year columns are exhausted involves wastage of time, money and energy.

9.2.4 *Stock-taking by Numerical Counting*

This is not a scientific method. In this method stock-taking may be made by mere counting of books on the shelves, on the charged trays (issue register), on the binding trays and other records, and by deducting the total number arrived at by numerical counting from the total number of books accessioned as per Accession Register except withdrawal book. The balance is the number of untraceable books. This method gives a rough idea of the books lost, but does not serve the basic purpose of stock-taking and does not give clear picture of library holdings.

9.2.5 *Computer Machines and Sample Stock Verification*

Computer machines are used for stock-taking work. In some cases only a few sections which are mostly in use are checked thoroughly and an estimate of the total loss is made on this basis.

Modern trend is stock verification by computer. This system is an accurate and foolproof. It is perfect and give proper result. But it is costly and not applied in all libraries in India as most of the libraries are not installed computers.

REFERENCES

Foskett, A.C. "Shelf Classification." *Lib. Jrl.* 95, 1970.

Rider, R. *Compact Book Storage.* New York, Hadham Press, 1949.

Sharma, C.K. *Dictionary of Lib. & Information Science.* Delhi, Shree, 2002.

Sharma, C.K. *University Library: Management and Organization.* Delhi, Metropolitan, 1977.

10

Library Rules

10.1 Introduction

Each and every library is governed by some rules and regulations for proper management and maintenance. All library authorities are empowered by Act to frame such rules as are necessary for their libraries. Different types of libraries will need different types of rules. Similarly rules are framed for academic or special libraries but it will not suit the purpose of a public library. Fundamentally the rules and regulations for libraries will have something common basically.

The modern age is no longer the age of librarianship. Books are no longer to be kept chained. Many modern libraries are of opinion that it is better to loose a few books yearly than to protect them by troublesome regulations from the few dishonest people in the community. Generally rules are framed to cover the following aspects — (a) Hours, (b) Holiday and Sunday openings, (c) Borrowing Rights, (d) Protection to property including mutilation of books, (e) Fines and Penalties.

Every library has its different types of readers. Academic library is related to courses and research, Technical and Business library deals with specific reader while Public library deals with all matters but more the general reading. Librarians are very careful about their responsibilities. They maintain discipline and create good atmosphere to attract a good number of readers. Library rules help the librarian and library staff in smooth running of the library. In fact stress is given upon the value and service that the library offers and to make the fullest use of the library.

Rules should be based on following factors:

1. Rules should be based on common sense.
2. Rules should be general for general reader.
3. Rules should be specific for specific readers.
4. Rules should be common to all.
5. Rules should be based on the aims and objects of the organization.
6. Rules should be based on the point of security of the library.
7. Rules should be easy to understand.
8. Rules should be in simple language of the area of library.
9. Rules should be based on social structure, culture and customs of the area as well as the nation.

Rules should be framed with the aim to strengthen the relations with the readers and minimize the red-tape. In our country this red-tapism often creates havoc and as a consequence the public are repelled from instead of being attracted towards, the library. Rules for the loan of books should be made for effective use of the books and get them and take them and not with the idea of finding some technical flaw which will make the enquirer ineligible. The sympathetic and ever helpful attitude of the library staff should be the golden rule in all libraries of our country and this alone should govern the relation between the library and its users. A librarian is always to be helpful to the reader and sympathy and not apathy is to be his guiding principle for all who approach him for help.

The discipline of the students in library is a most disagreeable task, but one which must be handled by the librarian, unless the seriousness of the offence requires that the problem be handled by the committee. The rules should be as elastic as possible in their codified form.

It is important that ordinary infractions be handled in a routine manner without favouritism or the granting of special privileges or without undue emphasis upon either crime or punishment. The librarian may levy fines as provided for in the rules, and restrict the use of the library to continually offending persons and/or even withdraw library privileges altogether. But the librarian must be careful not to exceed his authority.

Rules should be clear for following factors:

(a) The number of hours during which libraries remain open for service varies according to the local conditions, staff and funds. Local conditions and local needs have always to be kept in view. The principle of convenience of the clientele and the maximum use of the library have to be kept in view.

(b) Partial openings or Sundays and holidays are also very common in some places. Library openings should be left to the local authorities to decide. In case of public libraries in areas where the public are library minded and where maximum use of the library is possible, library closings should be kept to the minimum. Research libraries and university libraries at many places have opportunities for library work throughout the year and almost round the clock.

(c) In case of libraries all citizens have a right to use the library and borrow books for home issue. There are points in connection with the borrowing right of various classes of citizens. The borrowing right is generally extended without charge to householders, their families and to lodgers and other non-householding residents. Teachers engaged generally in educational work and serious students should be dealt with generously be lent as many books as they may need at a time.

(d) Personal effects should not be permitted in the libraries and these should be left with the janitor at the entrance. The Rules should allow maximum protection to all library property and all mutilation of book and damage to property etc. should be replaced at the cost of the reader or member responsible for such acts.

(e) Readers should use their own tickets for issuing books. In our country public libraries have no unlimited resource of books and so multiple number of books for home use is generally not done. One or two books are the usual practice.

(f) In case of delay in returning books the system of late fine and penalty for late return etc. is the accepted rule. But such fines should be levied with discretion. Specially in case of illness or where unavoidable cause of detention. The librarian has generally the power to excuse or reduce the penalty or fine payable for such delay in returning books.

(g) The period of loan is to be clearly stated. The abstracts of rules and the more important rules are often printed on the library ticket, sometimes these are printed and pasted on the back cover of book.

Areas of Rules: Libraries whether large or small should frame their own rules according to the nature and object of the organization. Rules should be framed in many categories so that these may be clear to understand and applied easily.

1. Rules for Library timings,
2. Rules for circulation services,
3. Rules for Reference service,
4. Rules for Reading rooms,
5. Rules for membership,
6. Rules for Inter-library loan service,
7. Rules for specific and rare reading material,
8. Rules for researchers,
9. Rules for duplicating the material,
10. Rules for computer service – Cyber café, Internet service, E-mail service etc.,
11. Rules for Acquisition of material,
12. Rules for Selection of reading material.

REFERENCES

ALA Committee on Code of Ethics, *ALA Bull.* 33; 128-30.

Board, J.C. *Charging for Public Libraries.* IFLA. 13, 4, 1987.

Gapp, K.S., "The Librarian taste in improving personnels." *Coll & Res. Lib.* 8, 1947; 427-35.

Sharma, C.K. *Modern Library Systems.* Agra, Y.K., 1990.

Sharma, S.C. "Raging the Library." *Lib. Jrl.* 66, 1941; 970.

Swank. "The Education Function of University Library." *Lib. Trend.* 1; 41-42.

11

Maintenance of Library Materials

It is very important to ensure correct shelving for giving efficient service to the library user *i.e.* delivering a book to a reader when it is wanted and restoring it to the assigned place in the shelves when it is no longer needed. Moreover, books in the stack shelves should be carefully preserved and making safe from dust, dirt, humidity, insects, fire etc. Shelf arrangement should be such that the most used books are brought near service points without too much disregard of the classification scheme. Oversized books should be specially shelved. Non-book materials are to be housed and arranged separately and in a suitable way. The moving and shifting of the collection should be properly planned and periodical inventory is to be made of the materials in the library.

In small library shelving work is done by the Circulation Department. In large libraries more staff are required and it would be advisable to have a separate department like the Shelving and Maintenance Department in charge of an Assistant Librarian.

11.1 Planning of Stocking

The stack area should be carefully laid out with the subject of accommodating books of all sizes as well as non-book material. Every volume should be planned to access to every volume and easy communication with other departments.

The stockroom should be well-ventilated, well-lighted, free of dust and with arrangements for temperature and humidity control.

Planning should be made for adequate provision for expansion either horizontally or vertically. The shelves should be attractive, functional, and durable and should be designed to accommodate the maximum number of materials in minimum amount of space and properly guided in a continuous days. On normal fixed shelves materials can be arranged in double rows. Bracket stacks are also used. Bracket stacks consist of tabular columns, into which the shelf brackets are supported by a heavy shelf base and the shelves are easily adjusted at 1 inch intervals.

There are libraries adapted the multi-tier stacks *i.e.* a system constructed with a self-supporting metal framework extending from basement to roof, and designed to carry the weight of the books load, with the weight of the deck floors and line dead.

Rolling stacks: "Metal stack units mounted on wide tread ball-bearing wheels" were first used in India.

Compact storage: Compact storage system "consists of units of three stacks, the centre row of fixed double-sided stacks at each side. Each hinged stack is hung on ball-bearing pivots without rails or guides and is easily swung into the aisle to give access to material in the inner shelves".

How to shelve: Classified manner is most commonly used method of arranging books on the shelves *i.e.* according to a classification scheme used in the library. But it is not always possible to arrange books in the classified sequence. For physical reasons it is sometimes found necessary to have size grouping of quartos and folios, including atlases which cannot be placed with crown or demy octavos.

Reference books, children's books and local history collection may be placed separately in special sequences, sometimes the arrangement is not strictly according to the classified order.

Books of various sizes – octavos, quartos, folios on a particular subject are arranged on the same shelves, in such a manner that no space is wasted. The arrangement is classified, though the sequence is parallel.

Periodicals: There should be separate stack area for shelving bound periodicals, which may be kept in parallel shelves near the books on the related subjects. In big libraries periodical stack area is attached with periodicals department.

Maps: Maps are frequently used. Only few maps are normally used at large. All maps which are frequently used may be laid flat in a blue-print cabinet. Most used maps are put in a single folder or drawer so that they can be easily located, removed and refiled.

A map cabinet of 22" × 24" drawers may be used for filing maps horizontally and in alphabetical order, the height of the cabinet to be determined by the principle of easy accessibility. In general it should be about 6½ feet high from the floor level.

Pamphlets: Pamphlets may be kept in manila folders and filed in vertical file cabinets subjectwise. There should be periodical weeding of out-of-date and unused pamphlets to avoid unnecessary congestion. Pamphlets may be displayed according to their nature.

Films & microfilms: Such material should be kept in a specially built metal cabinet which will be inflammable. There are vertical files, or file boxes. But they need not be kept in classified order. Cabinet and files must be dust and dirt proof.

Physical upkeep: Every library is facing the problem of preservation particularly physical upkeep. Although the chief problems of physical upkeep will vary in different kinds of libraries. Rare books, most concerned with such matters are treatment of paper (cleaning, de-acidifying etc.), care of leather bindings, maintenance of correct atmospheric condition, and protection against pests, vermins, cockroaches, white ants, rats etc. Public and academic libraries where books are in constant use are more concerned about the processes of re-binding cleaning. This is a continuous process throughout the year. To maintain the physical upkeep regular there should be a policy framed and established on a professional level and methods and techniques to be used should be determined in respect of original material, microtexts, rare books and manuscripts.

Binding and repairing of books and non-book material is an essential process in library. There are books of different nature and a decision is taken which book require binding or repair and judgment is taken in weighing relative advantages of binding, repairing and replacement.

11.2 Binding and Binding Department

Binding: Books are generally published within a form of publisher's casing, that is "a light strawboard cover cloth binding. Each book is paper bound or hard bound. Moreover a jacket of superior polished paper is used as cover of the book". The deciding factors are: (i) the physical quality of the book itself; (ii) the permanent value of the content. A less obvious policy is to bind before necessary in order to obtain a longer ultimate life.

Various binding specifications are necessary for different classes of material, and their preparation requires a knowledge of material and techniques and their relative costs in relation to the value, use, and expected life of different types of items.

According to American Library Associations the specification should also include the schedule of prices for different sizes of books to be bound in (a) half-leather, (b) quarter-leather, (c) cloth (varieties to be specified), and (d) buckram. Prices of other sizes, and for lettering, mending torn or broken leaves, guarding plates, mounting and dissecting maps (for square foot) should also be mentioned.

Binding record: Binding record is maintained in each library but it is not the same. However, in large libraries, before giving the books for binding the following process is followed:

1. Books, to be given for binding should be selected on the basis of:
   (a) Condition of book
   (b) Use of book
   (c) For future precaution
2. Books should be bound:
   (a) In cloth if it is used rarely.
   (b) In leather, if it used heavily and hardly available in market and costly.
   (c) In rexin if is commonly used by a specific or a group of readers.

Binding Register

Name of the Library

Title____________________

Author____________________

Call No.____________________

Binding required: Leather/Rexin/Cloth

Colour required:____________

Other instruction____________

____

Date of giving books for binding____________________

Date of return of books____________________

Binder

Rate:

Leather________________

Rexin________________

Cloth________________

Address____________________________________

Phone:____________________

Binding Department: In most of the libraries particularly in small and medium size libraries, binding of books is given to outsider binder. There is no binding department. Few books are given for binding every year, which does not require separate binding section. Books for binding are collected by Acquisition Department and given to binder after proper entry in Binding Register.

In large libraries like University libraries, there is separate department of binding of books. It is a small department with 2 or 3 Book Binders with a senior as In-charge among them. In some libraries Assistant Librarian is given responsibility of this department.

Binding Department and its in-charge perform the following fuctions:

1. to maintain record of the binding of books;

2. to select the books for binding, and divide them in three categories:
   (a) Full binding (stand and binding)
   (b) Temporary or cloth binding
   (c) Repairing of books
3. work distribution of binders.
4. checking the standards of bound books.
5. maintaining close working relations with other departments.
6. formulation of policies covering building.
7. preparation of Binding budget.

12

Library Co-operation

12.1 Introduction

No library is perfect and sufficient to satisfy its clientele and unable to house all the collection required by the readers. It will be manifest that co-operation in every direction of library work will be conductive to proper book service and the allied service of supplying information which is now-a-days an essential part of a library work. Similarly all information and queries are not possible to be answered by the librarian in any library. Indeed information has to be gathered from different sources, not only from other libraries and librarians of other organizations but also from other outside sources. Besides, each and every librarians has to try his best to make good book selection and to make the most of his limited book purchase grant. Library husband his sources on the principle of best books at least cost for largest number. Thus co-operation is needed at each and every stage of library work and service. The main principle of co-operation is to facilitate easy supply of materials to the readers without increasing the book budget and avoiding unnecessary delay and saving the reader's time.

Co-operation means to handle the work or operation with other help. No one is monark and work single handled until unless he is helped by man or machine.

An ideal library service would be one in which every book in any library would be available if needed, without delay or complexity. Sometimes it is said that privatisation of libraries cannot serve the readers fully and libraries may be nationalised. It will also be not a solution. Libraries should be given in the hands of the proper person, organization and then the government. National library service is more useful for co-operative movement. All libraries are put in a network and co-operate each other in a automatic channel. System will have special reservoir of books wanted only sparingly, central book collection based on local demands, co-operative buying, publicity methods, reading lists, bibliographical films and talking-book collections.

British library system and public library system in some of Indian states are the examples of co-operative effort in which every library is an independent unit but in a network co-operation. All the libraries have a union catalogue and master catalogue.

The libraries of U.K. have been linked together, first into a services of regional group, which new cover nearly the whole Kingdom, with a storing library as the centre of each and finally by the creation of a National Central library which co-ordinates and assists. The whole work and binds it to a single unity. In India there is no such network at national level. The National network has many merits—

1. to supply on loan to libraries,
2. to supply on loan to readers,
3. to act as clearing house or exchange for mutual loans of such books between other libraries,
4. to act as bibliographic centre for national and international purpose,
5. to facilitate access of books and information about the books.

12.2 Library Extension Service

Libraries are not only book issuing centre only. Its main purpose is to provide library service to its clientele residing in any corner of the area country. The public library plays a far more important role in society than what it did a century ago. No librarian can feel satisfied with the work that the library has been doing so far as book service and universal use of the library is concerned. Though a library has thousands of members, there will certainly be many in the region who are potential users but who may not know or care to know of

INTER LIBRARY PROGRAMME

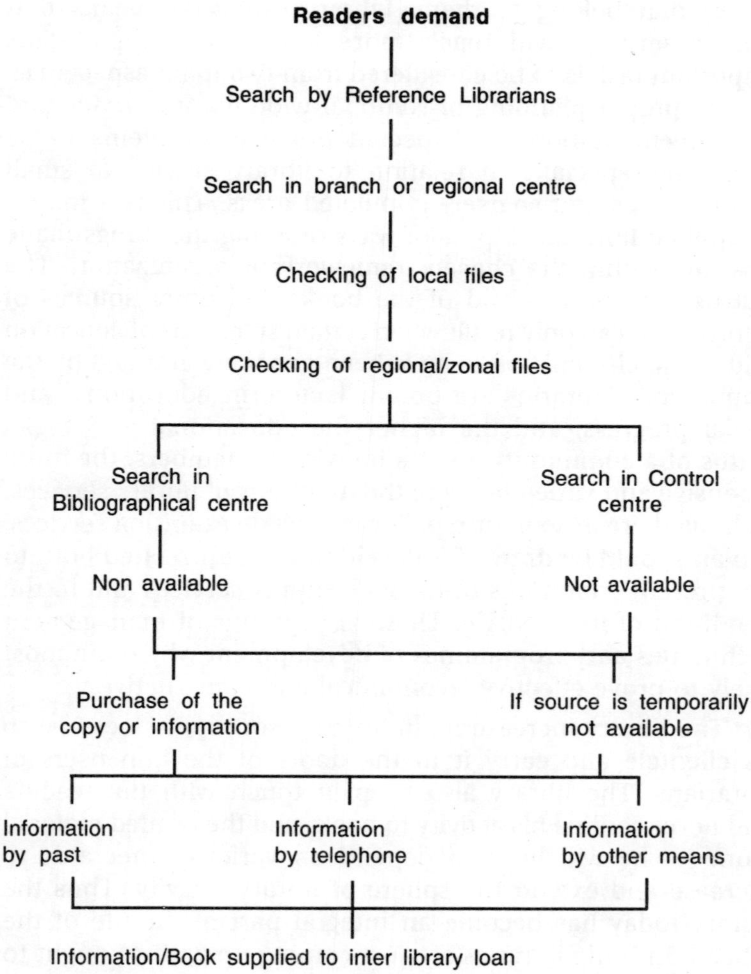

the existence of the library and the facility that the library offers other than those in the shape of book service. According to Mr. McColvin, the phrase library extension is understood differently in different countries. It means the extension of the normal work of the library to other related and associated fields, such as lectures, exhibitions, film displays, musical and dramatic activities etc. for children and adults. The proper function of the library is the development and enrichment of life in the entire community by bringing to all the people the books that belong to them. Library extension means that library services will reach more and more people. This important task is to be considered from two main aspects *viz*: (a) the proper planning of National wide library service and its implementation (b) Expected practical problems to be overcome, specially in relation to library service to small communities and sparsely populated areas. This is a matter of applied librarianship — of ways of doing the things made possible within the chosen framework or organization. The full use of libraries and of the books and other sources of information can only result when certain standards of education and social circumstances have been generally attained by the population. Libraries are potent factors in educational and social progress, and the higher the educational and social status of a community and its individual members, the more extensive and varied become the functions of library services. In India there is no inform policy to provide extension services. A plan should be drawn for development best related both to the present conditions of its book supply services and to the condition of its clientele. There are systems of management techniques and programmes of development which are most likely to prove effective, economical and constructive.

The library increase its utility and convey its message to its clientele and carry it to the doors of the non users of librarians. The library also keep in touch with the readers and never confine his activity to books and the printed material alone — he will have to depend on various other aids to increase and extend the sphere of library activity. Thus the library today has become an integral part of the life of the citizen. In India libraries are just coming up and we ought to learn by the experience of the other countries and should avoid all the unwanted mistakes they had committed to ensure our progress to be sound and quick.

The librarians both in our country and for years together in the west that there are many in the community who do not use their libraries. In the developing countries there are few literates in the villages and rural areas there is provision for the rich assortment of non-book materials *i.e.* recordings, radio-transcriptions, motion pictures, filmstrips and lantern slides, television etc. which seem to offer a partial solution of the problem. The use of such non-book materials is new and we have to be cautious in judging their adaptability to our needs and conditions. The use of non-book materials was made at first to act as lures to reading, but later on it was discouraged when circulation records failed to show immediate results. Audio-visuals materials can never take the place of books. They should not be considered as devices for building up the circulation of books. They are useful in themselves, but not for stimulating much more reading of books. Neither should they be used merely to divert with sound and motion. They can enrich the library's book services by supplementing them on take information and ideas to large numbers of people whom books are not reaching. By increasing the collection and intensity of the library "services library multiply its community contacts and increase its effectiveness". Audio-visual material requires clear understanding of the effects they produce.

The library has to provide materials for a lifetime reading which requires the library stock to be kept upto date. Readers may find the readers' material regularly. Ambitious need readers books and always trace new books. All librarians of libraries have to realise that their libraries should be able to do more than meet the existing needs. They should be able to help to improve and extend their services. They should, within their inevitable limits, be a demonstration of the wealth, range and variety of the world of books and encourage people to use them. Good book stock is an essential need and it is more important to have the books exploited or properly serviced.

The main purpose of library extension to make books useful to people and attract them for more reading and keep in touch with the library. Library management should understand the everyday routines and techniques of effective librarianship which means that trained and experienced staffing is obligatory. The importance of qualitative staffing is once more stressed.

All library services should be as good as it is possible to make them. Inadequate libraries achieve little whereas good libraries can achieve almost anything. People will always use good libraries to the full only because they are useful. Both the people and the government will support those libraries that are both useful and in demand.

Our authorities should be properly guided in their efforts to embark upon library provision or to develop services. In most of the developed countries where library systems have been established early there are eager critics anxious to remove limitations due to the accidents, mistakes, misconceptions, inherent in the process of growing up. Any sound library extension programme pays heed first to the conditions in which it must operate, secondly to the lessons of history and thirdly to certain basic principles. Library extension is a process of creating and increasing library resources and of securing their use. A library system or a national library service cannot be built up overnight by the waving of a magic wand. The entire system is an organization which needs nurturing to enable it to grow up — gathering strength and influence stage by stage.

12.2.1 *Factors*

1. Understanding: A library service is projected or an existing one is to be improved. People should visit and study existing services, discuss ideals and objectives with those concerned before they plan for their own purpose and should know what has been attempted and how.

2. Staff: There should be a provision of suitable staff. The staff determine both the rate and the quality of progress, sufficient suitably experienced and qualified personnel to man the libraries book services.

Once the libraries are well established, the personnel must be recruited and trained specially for library work. It is essential to selecting the best available people on the basis of personal qualities, abilities and sociability. Second, librarians to other countries to study developed library services, to study conditions, to attend library school course, to work in libraries, learn how to tackle their problems and when they have learnt. Established state or national schools to train further personnel of various grades — staffed by those sent abroad, perhaps with the assistance of teachers and experts, starting in-service training and also evening classes for working librarians.

All these process has three implications: (i) service agency is to be manned by some men with the maximum possible experience, (ii) must be the maximum mobility of staff, and (iii) must be closely related to the rate of staff production. Staff mobility in the library or one library to other libraries may be useful and give variety of knowledge, experience and efficiency leads to greater responsibilities. This also enables to the staff to enjoy variety of work and acquire a wide understanding of the problems of library service and thus makes librarianship an attractive career.

3. The invitation: Library staff should how desire to participate or the local initiative is very necessary. Any effective library service must be both suited to and the expression of the community rooted in the individual and the locality concerned, it cannot be imposed from above but must be desired by the people and their governments, both local and state. Extension service should proceed step-by-step at the local regions and other centres step-by-step. The rate of growth is to be gradual, some regions or centres will enjoy the fruits first, some next and so on. The extension work has to start under the best auspices and so become the best demonstration and the best encouragement for other authorities. It is the local initiative and the desire of the people for better and more services that will decide the ultimate steps in introducing library extension programmes.

4. Eradication of illiteracy: Staff, equipments, and service points will be few or many according to the total resources available for distribution. Library services and extension work be more than the actual resource position can justify the result will never be encouraging as the inevitable result of such a process will mean the founding of many inadequate and useless libraries. It is truth that without adequate resources proper functioning of an useful service can never be feasible and hence on the furnishing of adequate resources all extension work will necessarily depend.

Libraries are of no use if there are no readers. There are people who can but won't read and there is also another category of people who would like to read but are not equipped and hence cannot read. It is true where there is a high percentage of illiteracy it is useless to expect the same amount of library use. The literate population in illiterate areas will need more libraries and not less libraries, because their responsibilities as citizens and their opportunities as leaders and educators is to be greater. The variety, quantity and the range of materials required will also be not very different in these two cases. Everywhere where there will ultimately be need for full library service points there should, as the extension programme develops, be collections of material appropriate for and attractive to the neoliterates. This aspect of provision of adequate literature according to the needs of the newly made literates is a special feature for all rural library centres. Our libraries are to work in close association with the other educational agencies.

12.2.2 *Non-Book Materials*

Modern libraries are well equipped with non-book materials are providing service. The most important of such materials is Phonorecords which have played a very important role in library extension work. The music discs or gramophone records, taperecords now-a-days have been of a great variety. Internet and E-mail/Commerce services are modern developments.

The learning of Hindi and other Indian languages in the same process may be experimented upon. Public libraries have begun to use wire or tape recordings of important broadcasts, local events and their own programmes also. This practice is gradually being adopted in many of our libraries also.

12.2.3 *Motion Pictures*

One of the important media of mass communication is the motion picture. The use of this medium of mass contact has been very systematically done during the last two decades also with wonderful result. The latest trend is to run film libraries wherefrom local organizations may borrow films for display amongst their members.

Libraries are most forward in adopting mechanical aids.

One finds the use of films in all possible projects not only for discussion groups, but also for parents groups, young people's organizations, libraries help other agencies to develop their own programmes by advising on the choice of films and by providing opportunities for pre-viewing. Film shows at hours convenient for busy people are weekly, sometimes daily events in bigger libraries. Films along with other audio-visual aids have a very big future for library extension work in our country specially when illiteracy still plays a big part in public life in the rural.

12.2.4 *The Radio*

The Radio of the wireless broadcasts have begun to make headway in all country. The radio has a very bright future for library extension and development in any country, because it has a much wider audience and can appeal to many at a time — both literate and illiterate. Broadcasting programmes should be drawn up in consultation with experienced librarians, authors and people in the allied profession including teachers. The latest case in the developed countries is for television, which has been slowly and steadily making headway in most of the countries also. Well-throughout telecast programmes will surely help libraries and adult-education programmes. The education services of telecast programmes lie in the future. Libraries can afford television sets and are providing more educational programmes. Indeed much can be done by co-operation between libraries with tele-sets and television stations. The television stations use the library's television audience as critics of its programmes. Television stations have in many places featured "Great Books", discussion groups, forums and lectures on serious subjects. Libraries have been allowed to co-ordinate television programmes with educational films.

Stations have in many places featured "Great Books", discussion groups, forums and lectures on serious subjects. Libraries have been allowed to co-ordinate television programmes with educational films.

12.2.5 *Audio-Visual Aids*

Much spade-work and foundation work in book service is being done according to well set out plans under proper supervision. Organizing of cultural shows, local exhibitions, lectures by important men of the locality, talks on current problems etc. may all be periodically used for library extension programmes. The use of epidiascopes, films, film strips and lantern slides etc. are modern innovations and are useful vehicles for mass contact.

There are few libraries organizing the book service and also looking into and expending their services more and more with the help of various internal and external aids. Library extension is largely concerned with the scope and quality of book stocks and with the places to which people go and these places are provided with books and staff. These places are known as service points — and they have an almost infinite variety ranging from the huge central libraries of the metropolis to libraries on wheels, books delivered by the mobile. There are organized library service, such terms as library on wheels and may not properly be understood by the common man.

12.2.6 *Book Stock*

All agree that larger the book stock and better the staffing the greater is the satisfaction to the readers and higher is the quality of reading as well. It is unwise to encourage readers to be satisfied with an inadequate stock of books. Multiplication of such handful stocks of books, though seemingly convenient, ultimately impedes founding of efficient libraries or financial grounds — not to speak of other reason.

12.2.7 *Building*

Building can come later on where on the one hand, the authority knows but from experience where to site the library and on the other has a reasonable idea of how big it should be. It is a common fact that most libraries built at the outset from either too big, in which case they are a heavy inability.

Use of modern fluorescent lighting where possible will not only be economical in the long run, but will also improve the brightness of the library. The librarian in all library centres should have an eye for beauty. A small garden, 'flower bed, a green spot round the library in the rural areas will surely add to the aesthetic sense of the staff'. Book mobile play an important role in library extension work.

12.2.8 *Mobile Van*

Under the Five Year plans provisions the District libraries have been provided with mobile libraries wherever feasible. Thus library vans are not always full-fledged moving libraries with works displayed on the shelves but are generally country type vans which serve all purposes. Library service have to organize their book mobile services on very sound principles. Efficiency will depend upon proper utilization of the opportunities offered through the mobile units to the people in the scattered and far flung areas. The library vans should be more or less of multipurpose type for our purposes and will be giving more service for carrying exhibition materials as also audio-visual implements.

12.2.9 *Library Publicity*

Sometimes libraries are not properly used due to ignorance of service, prejudice or misconceptions and absence of desire to use books. Reading materials have an appeal to literates everywhere. Interesting programmes of lectures and use of audio-visual implements championing the good effects of reading and progress through knowledge from books will all go to increase the desire to read and use books.

Book displays and exhibitions and demonstrations of library facilities arranged in connection with teacher's conferences, public health demonstrations, local folk festivals will both serve the publicity purpose of the library as also the more important function. The library primarily exists for helping the people in their individual and community interests and thus encourage all possible organized groups and associations to publicise the library by adopting it as a means of promoting their own particular interest. Such advertisement or publicity work done from outside the library has the advantage of reaching new potential readers also.

The librarian has to play an important role in the fostering of such local associations and enthuse the interested persons to meet together and discuss the common aims. The library in every case becomes a popular centre and meeting ground of the cultured people of the locality. The library may invite the co-operation of the relevant government departments in the matter of participation in their meetings of the people with similar interests and thus gain much knowledge which ordinarily they may not have.

Public library centres play an important part in the matter of entertainment of the local people through play acting and play reading groups. The library staff also participate in such displays and try to make the library an entertainment centre also.

The public library as the centre for diffusion of all artistic, educational, scientific and cultural development of the locality must have a universal appeal for all irrespective of age, sex, creed or class. Library today is the only institution which helps in raising the cultural level of the common man whether it is school, college or university and public library. The public library is said to be the people's university. As a friend, philosopher and guide in all problems of life, both individual and collective, the position of the library will be unique.

12.3 Campus Relations

Library is a social institution and its every work and service is related to society. Library is a co-operative effort at every level *i.e.* Administration, faculty and readers, youth and associations. All these factors are directly or indirectly related to the library and facilitated by the library service. Every library has its campus whether public, academic or special library.

Campus relations can be categorized into classes —

I. On Campus relations;

II. Off Campus relations.

12.3.1 *On-Campus Relations*

The basic objective of the university education is to produce qualified and able youngmen and women for the country. Librarian provides library service to the students with co-operation of faculty members. The library is judged by that it has the community, how it meets the community needs and what the community thinks about. The community served by the university library consists of the teachers and the students. It is the object of the library to collect necessary reading material prescribed in the courses of study, to collect reference books, periodicals and all other records thought necessary for informative and supplementary reading, to organize and promote use of the available materials.

Library relationship with the students is conducted mainly through the loan service, reference service, seminars, debates, and the student library committee or the participation of students in library committee. Library is an agency of education and should conform to the over all pattern of education approved by the university.

Library-student relations are inevitable in university. If there is no co-operation between the library and the reading community, the objective of the library as well as the higher education will fail. Indian universities have library committees which are represented by the faculty, teachers and the administrators. Students are not allowed to participate in library committee. Though this practice is not so rigidly followed as few universities have allowed students' participation like Delhi and Benaras Universities. The Kothari Commission (1964-66) and the Gajendragadkar Committee (1971) in education field, have recommended the student participation in the library committees. Student library committees may also be device for encouraging friendly associations and for understanding the use of library by the students.

Library committee pays an important role in the development of university libraries. It helps in the field of communication, finance and the student discipline. There should be a proper communication between the students and the staff. The committee helps the library staff to know the difficulties of students in consulting the library resources. Necessary suggestions are also given to the librarian by the committee from time to time. Libraries are not put on the list of financial relaxation. Each library has limited funds. Student library committee put its suggestions within the financial limits and collect money for library by the media of charity shows, and variety programmes.

Faculty relationship: "The libraries in higher education are facing pressure both internal and external for new and better services. Participative management is successful approach for university libraries. Subject specialists or the faculty members are the best co-ordinators in educational field. The relationship between the faculty members and the library staff should be strengthen and proper communication should be established. Faculty participation is an active approach in library management. Library committee are constituted with faculty members and the administrative authorities. They are in a large number in library committee and discuss the various administrative and financial problems of the library. Subject specialist share the responsibility of selling the library service to its users. The communications between the subject specialist and users seriously effect the functioning of academic library service. Book selection is mostly controlled by the departments or faculties, which establishes direct communication between the department and the library.

Relationship is influenced by two things: Kind of service of library staff and their work. The librarian works in close relation with departmental heads in preparing the budget allocation for books. Faculty library committee discuss and formulate library policies which effect both the parties.

Every public library has its area of service *e.g.* City library, Municipal library, District library, Regional library, State library and National library. They have their relation with their clientele of the area. The library nominate members out of community and society in different fields like labour, educated, illiterates, service personnels, researchers, businessmen etc. for library committee to keep in touch with them and aware with their reading problems.

12.3.2 *Off Campus Relations*

12.3.2.1 *Academic Library*: There are some agencies which do not stay on the campus but the library needs relationship with them, because they stimulate personal or professional growth. Such agencies may be categorized as under:

1. Alumni group of library users;
2. Library Associations.

1. Alumni group of library users: Alumni group is important and helpful to the university and Special library. We call the alumni the sympathizers or the persons interested in the growth of library activities. University and research library provide reference service and provide bibliographical information to the users of off-campus. Publicity for gifts may take the form of direct appeals to individual alumni for special purchases or the publication of lists of desiderata in the alumni magazine. Alumni magazine is the best source to remind and refresh the memory of the persons who have been out of the university for the last several years and now forgotten all about the library. The magazine should contain some columns for special features of alumni's interest which can help to build up interest and goodwill to the alumni group.

Actually, there are persons, professors, laymen who have left the universities and institutions and are living a leisured life but are dedicated to the growth and improvement of the library as a repository for knowledge and literature. The relationship between the alumni group and the library staff is very much helpful for making library service efficient. Suggestions may be invited from the alumni group for the better management of the library. If this group is simply a show piece to the librarian, its value is lost.

There should be some rules and regulations for alumni groups which should include the service programme of the library, the ways of receiving aid from the alumni. Gerould says — "the library now is, what it is doing, that it desires to become, and how its friends can aid in its progress towards that goal". American Library Association issued a bulletin entitled, "Friends of the Library Group" university and college edition which described some rules and regulations, rules for alumnis and also published a list of material used by alumni association.

2. Library Associations and Organizations: The librarian is supposed to be a man who keeps in touch with all the associations, and the organizations, and the societies. Tauber has categorized the association as under:

1. Library Associations (Local);
2. Library Associations (National);
3. Learned Societies;

4. Educational Associations; and
5. Government Departments.

Several associations emerge and disappear frequently. But there are few important associations in the professional, academic and the cultural field which have more important role in the development of university library. They are listed below:

(i) American Library Association;
(ii) British Library Association;
(iii) Indian Library Association;
(iv) Indian Association of Special Libraries and Information Centres;
(v) State Library Associations;
(vi) District Library Associations;
(vii) Indian Publisher's Association;
(viii) Associations of Administrators, and the Adult Education, University Teachers, Indian National Library, Indian Science Congress, Indian History Congress, etc.

Library Associations are helpful in forming the working and sound management of a library. They have several ways of co-ordinating the various national and internal agencies. They participate in the service programme of the library through the following means:

(i) by developing the international programmes for the cultural activities;
(ii) by developing the educational programmes for the librarians;
(iii) by helping in the technical operation of reclassification and re-cataloguing by way of giving technical advice;
(iv) by helping in the compilation of major catalogue and union catalogues;
(v) by accomplishing other agencies of repute who are interested in promotion of research and advancement of scholarship in the field of library science;
(vi) by creating library consciousness among the public and also professional aptitude among the professionals, and

(vii) by improving the service conditions and the status of the librarian.

There are about 150 library associations all over the world. The first library association established was American Library Association in 1876 and was followed by British Library Association in 1877. In India, State Associations were established first and National Association afterwards. We can list the first five associations in India chronologically as under:

1. Andhra Provincial Library Association	1914
2. Bengal Library Association	1927
3. Madras Library Association	1928
4. Punjab Library Association	1929
5. Indian Library Association	1933

Associations may be divided in three categories: local, state and national. There are two national library associations in active service in India: I.L.A. and IASLIC.

12.4 Study Centre

University Grant Commission agreed to a proposal submitted by an Ad-hoc Committee appointed by it sometimes ago on the establishment of study centres in Indian universities. These centres were established with the aim to provide essential library facilities to the students in the residential areas. In the new established universities the university library is rather far from the residential area and it is difficult for the students of residential area to visit the university library. The other main reasons are: that it encourages the students living in the cities; it develops the habit of studies and thus saving the time. Library facilities provided in these centres include multiple copies of the textbooks in considerable demand. These centres serve as reference libraries where students consult the books in their reading hall. The scheme to establish study centres was implemented in the Fourth plan.

These centres were established as an independent unit of the universities managed by independent Managing Committees of the persons in residential area. The study centres may be managed by the university, colleges in their respective areas and local committee constituted to look after the working of the centres. The Managing Committee may consist of Principals, professors of the local colleges to served. The study centre committee should be set up in order to manage the affairs of the study centre.

The Managing Committee is vested with the powers necessary to run the study centre smoothly, which include the power of administering all endowments for the study centre and allotment made in the budget for purpose of books and periodicals or for general purposes of the study centre, allocating the funds for books among the various subject, laying down the procedures for selection and purchase of books and journals, preparing the budget of the study centres for consideration of the executive council, submitting to the executive council an annual report on the working of the study centre, framing rules for use of books and journals in the study centre.

Though University Grant Commission has not laid down any regulation for consisting the study centres and also the role of university librarian in the functioning of study centres. But it has closely mentioned that study centres will be managed by a local managing committee. It shows the clear intention of the U.G.C. to run the study centres independently and separately from the university libraries. But most of the universities have not constituted the local committees and centres are put under the direct control of the university librarian.

Book Selection: Study centres have not adopted a uniform pattern of book selection policy. Generally study centres are doing this work independently. On the other hand some study centres borrow books from the university library. Moreover, the books are purchased within the book budget of the centres by the university library and rolled out to the study centre. There are some study centres which are adopting the democratic pattern and following the Ranganathan's Concept of Books for All, by All! Each member of teaching department in local colleges is invited to suggest the better and suitable books of the particular subject for the benefit of the students he teaches at all levels. Such suggestions are scrutinized and checked against the holdings of the centre and sent to the professors of the different subjects for final scrutiny and recommendation and then approved by the chairman of the study centre or the managing committee.

At present study centres are facing accommodation problem. The policy of establishing the study centres is no doubt appreciable, but the U.G.C. should also provide sufficient funds for their accommodation. These centres should be run under the direct control of the U.G.C. and fully financed by it so that this library may serve the student community free of hand and with all reading facilities. By the time the central university libraries and departmental libraries have been developed and U.G.C. has not provided sufficient funds, study centres are lossing their objectives. Many study centres have been closed and merged with university libraries.

Management Setup of Library Staff

Library is a family of library staff with librarian as Head of the family. Each and every family member or the staff member of a library is supposed to be free from exploitation by the authorities or any individual. There should be personal relations among the staff members. A profession is a brotherhood. Professional activities and the participation of every staff member in such activities is desirable. All common interests and problems lead to a group consciousness which improves the efficiency in the library profession. There are several factors which foster inter-relationship and strengthen it.

Library Staff Room: Industry and the business enterprises are always mean to take the working conditions of the workers more attractive and comfortable. Staff room facilities are accorded where all staff members collect together and chit-chat on various individual and the industrial problems as a whole. Libraries also provide comfortable staff room for the library staff. Well-lighted and spacious work rooms, adequate heating and ventilation, sound proofing, and up-to-date furniture and equipment go so longway in helping to secure and hold a satisfied staff. Staff room greatly contributes to the satisfaction of the library staff and conserve the strength of the personnel and build their morale. The necessity of the staff room is recognized by the modern libraries. Staff room solves various problems as it help in relaxing the tired worker during lunch hours and also serve as a meeting place for parties and discussions over common problems.

Staff Clubs: Staff recreation clubs have also proved more helpful in improving staff relations. These clubs organize various programme of social gatherings, occasional cultural programmes, parties, picnic, debates, lectures and other activities which develop group consciousness and are effective for good service. Staff clubs are also known as tea clubs. Staff members join together and enjoy tea in a group and discuss various problems through this media. Moreover, these clubs collect all staff members together and enable them to chalkout a programme for the welfare of the staff.

Staff Association: University library or large Public libraries' staff have staff association and the union to fight for their right cause. These staff associations are independent bodies and some affiliated to the university, institution or organization staff association. Phelps points out that "library staff unions have achieved limited success". Such staff associations are used as a plateform for carrying out group action. The status of librarian is not uniform in all the libraries. He may or may not be the member of staff association. If the librarian is not a member of the association, he is usually consulted in any action which convenes problem of internal administration. The staff association deal with the matters of faculty rank, tenure, promotions, retirement, — allowance, pension and gratuity facilities, representation at conferences, meetings, study leave, sick leave and salary protection etc. These associations also improve staff morale and undertake the work of publishing staff manual, hand books, and organizing professional libraries etc.

Staff Members: The librarian is always careful to develop good relations with staff members. He calls staff meetings frequently to solve library problems effecting the internal administration, and to clarify situations which involve inter-departmental relations. These meetings involve the whole staff of the library. In a big university library, separate meetings of section supervisors are held. Library meetings are presided by the university librarian. In addition to the meetings within a particular department are occasionally held when special problems arise. In university library staff meetings are held monthly, quarterly, half-yearly and yearly. The staff meetings provide good opportunities for exchanging views on various problems of procedures, service, personnel matters and also for introducing new methods, and changes in organization.

REFERENCES

ALA. Inter Library Code. *ALA Bull.* 11, 1977.

ALA Conference. Library Co-operation. 1971.

Ballar Singh, R.K. "Community Information Problems and Prospects in India." *Herald of Lib. Sc.* 26, 3-4, 1987.

Cox, P.J. "Lib. Co-operation and Co-ordination." In Sewell, P.H. *Five-year Work in Librarianship*. London, Lib. Asso., 1963.

Ewnig, N.J. "Borrowing from Our Neighbours." *Lib. Jrl.* 923, 193.

Garould, J.T. "Alumni and College Library." *ALA Bull.* Jan. 1936.

Green, S.S. "The Lending of Books to One Another by Libraries." *Lib. Jrl.* 1, 1976.

Hamilton, B.A. *Multitype Library Cooperation.* New York, Bowker, 1977.

Harrison, K.C. *Prospects for British Librarianship.* London, LA, 1976.

Jefferson, G. *Library Cooperation.* London, Andra Deutsch, 1977.

Irwin, R. *Golden Chain: A Study in History of Libraries.* London University, 1958.

Keshwani, K.S. "Opening the Library Exhibition." *ALA Bull.* II, 4, 1969.

Letheve, Jacques. "Project for standard book exchange request form." *Unesco Bull.* For Libraries. XXV; 5, 1971.

Lock, R.N. *Manual of Library Economy.* London, Clive Bingley, 1977.

Mahajan, S.C. "Resource Sharing and Networking of University Libraries in India." *University News.* 30, 1992.

Mandal, S. "Media and Marketing of Inf. Products and Services." *Coll. Libn.* 4, 1988.

Mitra, T.K. "New Dimensions of Library Science." *Herald of Lib. Sc.* 21, 3-4, 1982.

Mohan Rajan, P.A. "Relevance of 2nd and 3rd Laws of Lib. Sc." *ILA Bull.* 23, 1-2, 1987.

Nortier, M. "Inter Library Loan." *Unesco Bull.* For Libraries. 35, 1974.

Ranganathan, S.R. *Preface to Library Science.* Delhi University, 1948.

Shank, R. "Engineering Programs of Coop." *Lib. Trends.* 23, 1974.

Sharma, C.K. *Modern Library Systems.* Agra, Y.K., 1990.

Sharma, C.K. *University Library. Management & Organization.* Delhi, Metropolitan, 1977.

Staveley, R. "A Enquiry into Cooperation." *Jrl. of Doc.* 5, 1949.

Thomson, J. *History of Principles of Librarianship.* London, Clive Bingley.

Unesco. *Manifesto for Public Libraries.* Paris, UNESCO, 1972.

Urquahart, D.J. "The Ecolasy of Inter-library Loans." *Lib. Asso. Record,* 67, 1965.

Wilbour, S. *Mass Media and National Development.* Paris, UNESCO, 1978.

13

Communication and Co-ordination

13.1 Communication

Communication is the interaction of ideas, opinions or judgments, through the medium of speech, writing, broadcasting systems or other media which can be used for this purpose. In any organization communication is necessary if anything has to be done. The change is motivation, in attitude and in behaviour, is brought about by the leader through the communication. Communication is transmission and receipt, including comprehension of thought, instructions, or information. While we talk of communication in management in library, we analyse the world communication as to converse or transmit information from one person to the other. Basically, communication is a two-way process and two terminals should be concerned with mutual understanding if communication is to be purposefully effective.

Communication is giving and receiving information from two ways and through intermediate levels. Allen says: "Communication is the sum of all the things one person does what he wants to create understanding in the mind of another. It is bridge of meaning. It involves a systematic and continuous process of the telling, listening and understanding."

TOP WAY COMMUNICATION

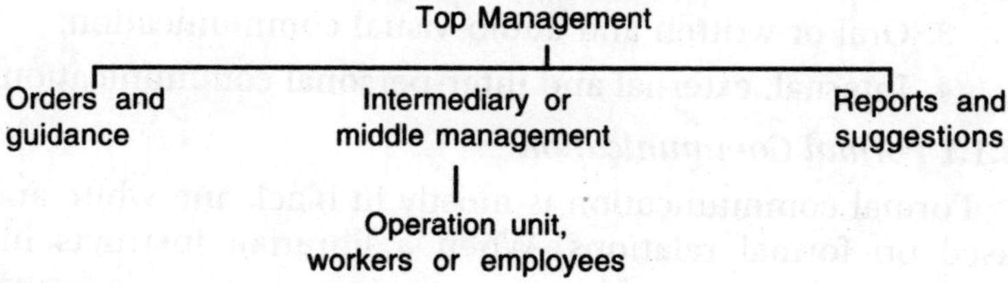

There are five elements constituting the communication process:

1. Communicator or sender — who possess necessary orders, guidance and instructions to the party or the next group, what to do.
2. Communication receiver or transmitter — who receives communication.
3. The message — which is transmitted and passes on by the sender to modify the behaviour of the receiver or communicator.
4. Communication channels or contracts among the top management and the individuals.
5. Response or reaction of the receiver.

In a library-management, librarian issues or sends necessary orders to the division/department/sectional in-charge or officers, who communicate them to the employees or workers of their sections. Here librarian is organ I, Sectional officers are organ II and employees are organ III. Organ I is communicator, Organ II is a communicational channel, orders and instructions are messages, Organ III is a receiver and the action or the work done by the receiver or the employees/ workers in a response.

Communication is an essential function of management. Good communication establishes co-ordination amongst staff members, which further results in securing concurrence and harmony in purpose and performance by intelligent team-work throughout the organization.

There are four forms of communication:

1. Formal and informal communication;
2. Upward, downward and horizontal communication;
3. Oral or written and audio-visual communication;
4. Internal, external and inter-personal communication.

13.1.1 *Formal Communication*

Formal communication is mostly in black and white and based on formal relations. When a librarian instructs his subordinate by virtue of his supervisory position, it is formal communication. Formal communication is passed through various levels of authorities.

13.1.2 *Informal Communication*

Informal communications are mostly free from all sorts of formalities. They are based on informal relations between the parties. It arises from the social and personal interests of the employee rather than formal requirements of an organization.

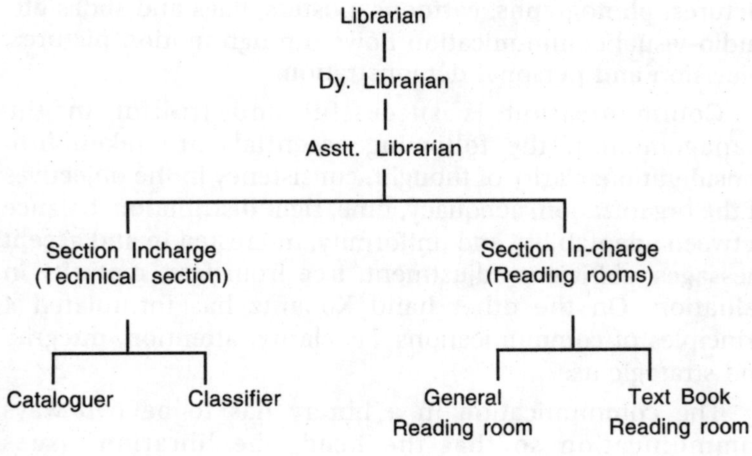

13.1.3 *Downward Communication*

Downward communication flow from upper level of management to the operative force. *Viz.* chief librarian to the last man in the library, while upward flows from the lower level to the uppermost level, *viz.* library clerks to chief librarian. Horizontal flows between two subordinates of the same ranks, *viz.* between two departmental heads or two technical assistants etc.

Downward	Upward	Horizontal
Directives	Reports	Reports
Manuals	Concerning work	Personal contacts
Orders	Requests for guidance	Staff meetings
Instructions	Suggestions	Co-ordination
Conferences	Discussions	Committees
Meetings		
Budget sanction		

13.1.4 *Oral Communication*

Oral communication flows face to face or through the telephone, while written communication flows through orders, instructions in writing. Oral communication is superior as it achieves better understanding and saves time. It carries more authority and leaves a record. Audio-visual communication leave more permanent impression on the audience. Visual media flows through circulars, manuals, reports, bulletins, pictures, photographs, cartoons, posters, flags and slides etc. Audio-visual communication flows through motion pictures, television and personal demonstration.

Communication is successful and fruitful in the management if the following essentials are taken into consideration: clarity of thought, consistency in the objectives of the organization, adequacy, time, right distribution, balance between adaptability and uniformity, interested in and accept messages, sufficient adjustment, free from fear, maturity in valuation. On the other hand Kooantz has formulated 4 principles of communications *i.e.* clarity, attention, integrity and strategic use.

The communication in a library has to be two ways communication so that the head, the librarian issues instructions, gives orders, sends messages to the subordinates and they understand them, follow them and comply them fully, and on the other hand whatever difficulty the subordinate faces is immediately communicated to the head for his consideration, review and action. Such two-way communication helps in maintaining order and discipline in the library.

13.2 Co-ordination

Co-ordination harmonizes all the activities of a concern in order to facilitate its working and its success. Proper co-ordination is essential for successful management. A co-ordinated operation is one in which the activities of the employees mere harmonious and integrated towards a common objective. Modern libraries depend on the specialization of functions and activities are delegated to different participating individuals. If each individual is allowed to perform his own functions efficiently without taking note of the connected function performed by another individually, the result will be chaos in organization. Hence complete co-ordination is needed. If the policy of co-operation and co-ordination is firmly established and each member of the staff is encouraged to regard himself and his work as vital to the whole organization, much will have been done to ensure efficient, interaction as well as personal happiness.

Co-ordination can be achieved by direct contact with the individual concerned, reciprocal relations, and continuous process. Co-ordination is not a easy task. It requires human relation, behaviour, adjustment and justified suggestions, guidance and the patience of bearing, grasping and understanding. The librarian has to try to maintain co-ordination among the subordinate staff. He makes all efforts to create atmosphere of brotherhood and organize occasional staff meetings to sort out their difficulties and seek their valuable suggestions. A feeling of co-operation and understanding is thus created and maintained.

There are various factors which are helpful in achieving co-ordination among the library staff:

1. Publication programme;
2. Staff council/meetings;
3. Staff manual;
4. Sectional meetings;
5. Staff ethics;
6. Limited control.

13.2.1 *Publication Programme*

The staff publication in the form of bulletin, handbills, pamphlets and staff guides etc. are used successfully to focus the staff activities. Such publications achieve co-ordination among the staff members. Some Indian universities have also published library staff reports, half-yearly or annually. Through such publications the authorities inform the staff members about professionals and their personal/individual activities, scholarly achievements and as such the activities of the whole library. The main purpose of staff publication is to express common interest and suppliment personal contact; to inform staff members of the professionals and personal activities; to relate the activities of the department; to record happening in the scholarly work.

13.2.2 *Staff Council*

Decentralization is beneficial on one hand but also defective on the other as it disrupts the library efficiency in a case of lack of co-ordination among staff members, overlapping of functions, superiority complex among senior staff and the false assumption of huge allotment of work in their section is a general tendency among some staff members. The defects may be recovered by way of organizing staff meetings and forming a staff council. Dr. Ranganathan says that staff behaviour and attitude may be co-operative if the members of the staff could be brought together by some system which could cultivate esprit-de-corps. He suggested the idea of staff council in 1932, "The librarian should meet the head of the sections at least once a month to discuss the various matters of inter-sectional adjustment." The formation of staff council and regular monthly meeting of the same will be helpful. The discussion with the staff of the main advancements in professional research, the development of techniques, policy, and educational objectives keeps alive interest in the newer phases of library science. The informal meeting through staff councils or so-called names 'friendly clubs', etc. has immensely enhanced the co-ordination programmes and thus working very satisfactorily.

13.2.3 *Sectional Meetings/Councils*

Sectional councils are also formed to discuss the problem of inter-sectional activities and the staff. These councils work as units of staff councils and meetings are held a few days before the meetings of library staff council.

13.2.4 *Staff Manual*

Staff manual is a common device of administration in a big libraries. It is simple method for making known the policies and practices in a large library and essential for effective service. Staff manual codify the policies and practices of library.

It has the following main functions:

1. It introduces the new staff member and his duties.

2. It assists a staff member to broden his point of view and stresses the educational objectives of the library.
3. It is a co-operative affair. It affords an opportunity for experience members of the staff to systematize and organize their work more effectively.
4. It promotes efficiency by insuring uniform procedures and determine responsibility.
5. It provides an effective media for interpreting the library to the administration with a view to enhance efficiency.

Staff manuals are generally of two types. General manual deals policies and practices of the library as a whole and departmental manual contains concrete and specific information about the work of the departments in question.

Fay has illustrated the following structure of the staff manual:

Title page		
Preface		
Introduction		
Administration	-	General regulations, staff recruitment, staff meetings, publicity publications, building.
Acquisition	-	General and exchanges and fifths, serials, accessioning, binding and repairs.
Cataloguing	-	and — Classification.
Circulation	-	General and reserve books, charging books, overdue fines, lost books, shelving.
Reference Service	-	Administration and organization of collection, routine and schedule, teaching service, inter-library loan, record and statistics.
Departmental Libraries	-	Organization, technical work.
Other services	-	Brosing room, seminar, collection, service to alumni and town people.
Index		
Appendix	-	Sample forms for all process, library supplies and source of purchase.

Manuals are not static instruments of managerial instruction, and needs revision from time to time when found necessary. It should be cyclostyled in the first edition and printed when standardized. Staff manual should be edited carefully.

13.2.5 *Staff Ethics*

The library is not an independent entity but a part of the institute with which it is associated. The rapid development of library service and the subsequent increase in the library personnel have served to call attention to the duties and obligations of librarians. As such careful planning for organization and administration should be made to provide the most efficient service to the students and faculty members. This obligation place a responsibility of loyalty upon each members of the staff, from the chief librarian to the assistant. A.L.A. adopted a code of ethics in 1929 in which several suggestions were advanced. The code emphasizes that librarians cannot act as isolated individuals in their work. The main suggestions were:

1. The librarian should perform his duties with realization of the fact that final jurisdiction over the administration of the library rests in the officially constituted governing authority.
2. The chief librarian should keep the governing body informed about the professional standards and progressive section. Each librarian should be responsible for carrying out the policies with a spirit of loyalty to the library.
3. The chief librarian with the help of the staff members should study the present and future needs of the library.
4. Librarian should be known to make the resources available to the potential users.
5. Impartial service should be rendered to all who are entitled to use the library.
6. It is librarian's obligation to keep secret the information received from the patrons.

7. The librarian's obligation to protect the library property and inculcate in users a sense of their responsibility for the preservation.
8. The chief librarian should delegate authority, encourage a sense of responsibility and initiative on the part of the staff members, provide for their professional development and appreciate good work.
9. A librarian should never enter into a business dealing on behalf of the library which will result in personal profit.
10. A librarian should never turn the resources of the library in his personal use.
11. Librarian should have a sincere belief and critical interest in the library profession.
12. Librarian should participate in public and community affairs.

For efficient management each head should have few persons under his control. There should be sectional officers responsible for the control of their sections. If there are more members of sections, few intermediary of channels should be appointed *i.e.* Deputy Librarian or Assistant Librarian. The same pattern should be adopted if more persons are in one section. Each section may be divided into more sections with separate incharge who will control few assistants of his sections:

CONTROLLING PROGRAMME OF LARGE LIBRARY

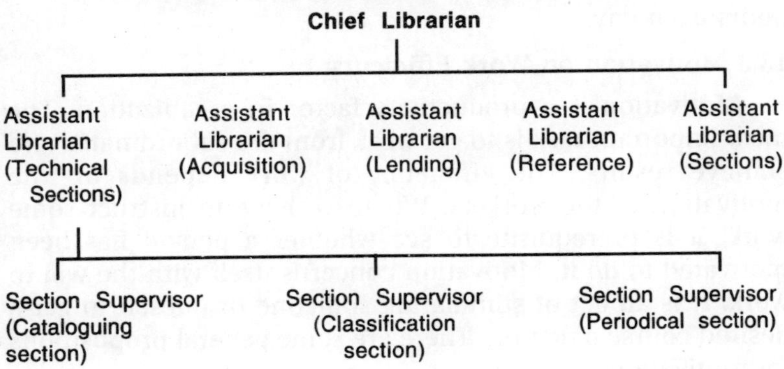

CONTROLLING PROGRAMME OF SMALL LIBRARY

Librarian

- Assistant Librarian (Technical Section)
  - Sections (Section Heads)
- Assistant Librarian (Public Services)
  - Sections (Section Heads)

Library conduct in-service programmes which are more useful as it endures continuity of the objectives, policies and services of a particular library and also helps in stimulating morale. The policy to give "equal pay for equal work" and the gradation of salaries in terms of demonstrable degrees of work difficulty or responsibility are essential to a sound personal system. Library employees should inculcate reading habits, Reading begets knowledge. More knowledge will improve the working and result in increased efficiency.

There is also a variation in the number of hours that libraries are kept open for the use of the students and faculty. The timings of circulation section as well as reading room are generally the same. Reading rooms are open on Sunday also for a limited service. It is also necessary to depute the professional heads on duties on Sunday if the library is playing its part in developing reading habits. According to A.L.A. standard the library should remain open for the period not exceeding 37-48 hours or as medium of 39½ hours per week for 1000 enrolment. But now library remain open even 10 hours each day.

13.3 Motivation on Work Efficiency

Motivation is a productivity factor in organization. The most important task is to get work from the subordinates and achieve results. The efficiency of work depends on the motivation of the workers. When we have to instruct some work, it is prerequisite to see whether a person has been motivated to do it. Motivation concerns itself with the will to work. It is an act of stimulating someone or oneself to get a desired course of action. There are some general propositions for motivation.

1. Motivation comes from inside; each individual's fundamental need; air, food and shelter etc. is goal directed and is purposeful.

2. The whole individual is motivated, not just part of him.

3. Frustration of basic needs makes a man "stick".

4. Basic need take effect motivators on different levels, the higher the level of the need, the greater is power to give enduring satisfaction.

The following factors are involved in motivation and work efficiency:

(a) Will to do work;

(b) Incentives capacity;

(c) Discipline;

(d) Clear understanding;

(e) Similarity in nature;

(f) Adequate salary;

(g) In-service training;

(h) Reading habits.

The library staff cannot achieve efficiency unless he intends to do work: incentives are taken, concentrates his mind towards his work, maintains discipline. Moreover similar work should be allotted to each groups of sections of the library. New staff members also inducted with certain devices of knowledge and library activities. Professional training includes providing professional literature instituting plan, reading courses, special meeting, group discussions and conferences. The members of one department are given the job of other departments. Facilities are extended to every librarian members and the qualified person is allowed to apply for particular high position.

REFERENCES

Allen, R.K. *Org. Management Through Communication.* New York, Harper, 1977.

Bell, D. "Communication Technology." *Eco Impact.* Feb. 1982.

Blagder, J.F. "Communication." *Aslib. Procgs.* 27, 1975.

Chandler, G. *Libraries in Modern World.* Oxford, Pergamon Press, 1965.

Cortez, E.M. "Communication as library management." *Jrl. of Lib. Adm.* 8, 1987.

Davis, Keith. *Human Relations at Work.* New York, McGraw Hill, 1962.

Goldberg, M. "Communication, Perception and Motivation." *Spl. Lib.* 51, 1960.

Gellerman, S.W. *Management of Motivation.* New York, Am. Management Asso., 1968.

Hodnett, Edward. *The Art of Working with People.* New York, Harper, 1959.

Johnson, Elmer. *Communication.* N.Y., Scarcrow Press, 1955.

Lovenstein, Aarson. *Why People Work.* New York, Crowell Callier, 1962.

Mahajan, S.C. *Resource Sharing and Networking in University Libraries in India.*

Maslow, A.H. *Motivation and Personality.* N.Y., Harper, 1954.

Mc Calvin, L.R. *The Chance to Read.* London, Phoenix, 1956.

Sethi, Atma Ram. "Communication in Libraries." *Herald Lib. Sc.* VII, 1972.

Sharma, C.K. *University Library: Management & Organization.* Delhi, Metropolitan, 1977.

Stale, B. "Computers and Communication." London, Blakies, 1990.

White, Carl M. *Basis of Modern Librarianship.* Oxford, Pergamon Press, 1964.

Wilbour, S. "Mass Media and National Development." Paris, Unesco, 1978.

Wilkinson, J.P. "The Perycho-Organizational approach to staff communication in libraries." *Jrl. of Acad. Libnship.* 4, 1978.

14

Reference Department and Service

It is the service rendered by a librarian in aid of some sort of study, the reference librarian as an interpreter of library resources, and reference literature as dictionaries, encyclopedias, almanacs, catalogues, compends, and other books held in the library for consultation.

Reference work in all libraries often seems the same; many of the books are identical, and to some extent the library patronage overlaps. Reference librarians deal chiefly with undergraduates in college libraries and with graduates and research workers in university libraries and public in public libraries.

In the public library the demand made upon the reference librarian is for definite information for immediate use; the patron is seldom interested in learning the process of acquiring information by and for himself. It is the duty of the reference librarian to help the student to help himself, to show him how to find the material for himself. It is possible to build up each year on the work of the previous year. And the questions asked are in part, at least, a repetition.

First, that all readers should realize how far they can, with advantage, use the basic reference books and indexes commonly found in libraries.

Second, that readers should develop a reasonable facility for the independent use of reference materials in looking for information and in preparing term papers and other assignments.

The attainment of these objectives depends upon the availability of a competent staff, unburdened by too much routine and organizational duty, and capable of working in close harmony with the readers community.

The reference librarian or staff member responsible for reference service in the library is frequently of assistance to the instructor in problems connected with teaching and personal study.

14.1 Organization

The size of the library has a direct bearing on the organization of reference service. In the small library the reference work may be performed by the librarian himself, or by the members of his staff without a definite departmentalization. It is estimated that only thirty-five of three hundred libraries had one or more persons devoting their full time to reference work. While making analysis of the organization in twenty-six large libraries, it was found that separate reference departments in half the libraries is working a combined reference and circulation department in five libraries and no special reference unit in four libraries. Reference department reaches its ultimate perfection when it is given separate departmental status.

The reference competency and skill that come from long experience in working with a restricted subject collection are well-known. Reference librarian should become a specialist in the history and bibliography of a field, not through long experience as reference librarian in a restricted subject collection or through special subject matter training, but through systematic study of the literature of the field.

Reference work is a co-operative undertaking in any library and its object is to give exact information of help in using library materials. If a cataloguer, an order assistant, or a circulation assistant is the best person to answer a particular question, his special knowledge should be utilized. Organization does imply, however, that the primary responsibility for reference should be definitely placed in every library.

The organization of reference service should have as its primary object the promotion of efficiency in helping readers to use library materials.

Qualifications for Reference Services: To fulfil the duties of reference service in a library, and to rise to the level of the opportunities which this work presents, the library assistant needs a somewhat formidable array of virtues. Industry, exactness, and a good memory are essential. Knowledge is not enough; on a par with knowledge and perhaps above it should be placed the ability to meet readers easily and to help them in a sympathetic, tactful way to stand on their own feet. Mental curiosity, imagination, and a sense of humour are desirable traits. Reference work is the very core and hub of a library service. It is the intermediary through which much of the work of other library departments is interpreted. Its usefulness should not be curbed by a too slavish adherence to regulations or a mechanical employment of the documents collected.

14.2 Reference Services to Readers

Reference service to readers is primarily an institutions problem and not merely a library problem. The teacher works under a distinct handicap when the reference librarian is not familiar with the purpose of class assignments; the reference librarian is limited in the help he can give readers without an alert faculty which requires, appreciates, and uses his knowledge.

Reference librarians, for their part, too often fail to realize that one of the things that can help their work in instruction is the habit of aiding readers to find what they want rather than actually finding it for them. When readers turn to the reference department as their first and last hope of getting material on the topics assigned them, the reference librarian should not immediately rush off to find the material, but should indicate where such material is likely to be found, and then let the student find it himself. "There are times when the librarian will best serve the interests and welfare of the readers by providing him with not only a completely worked out reference lists, but with the very books themselves neatly arranged on a table and topped with a little kindly note wishing him good luck". To promote bibliographic assistance, instructors should be urged to suggest to their readers that they register the topics of their term papers with the reference librarian as far in advance as possible of the time they are assigned. In this way, the library can purchase books and duplicates needed, arrange for guidance in the location of document and pamphlet material not accessible, or easily accessible, through the card catalogue and secure inter-library loans where needed. The library may properly take the initiative in preparing annual lists of source theme subject on which the library has an adequate supply of materials in various forms ranging from the encyclopedia to the pamphlet.

The test of the library's usefulness in answering information and fact-type reference questions is the ability of the staff to see that readers get the information they want or the knowledge of where to get it as quickly and as precisely as possible. It is dangerous to generalize from a few instances, but it would sometimes appear that reference librarians err in giving the reader more information than he needs or wants. These librarians suffer from an absolute excess of zeal. In their desire to be helpful, they forget for the moment that the function of quick information service is to save the reader's time.

14.3 Reference Librarian

Reference librarian is supposed to be a scholar, man of learning and book lover. He should have a knowledge of bibliographies and other reference tools. Reference librarian should inherent the following qualities:

1. He should be learned person;
2. He should be a professional having professional qualification;
3. He should have a quality of a teacher *i.e.* conversion ability;
4. He should have a quality of a critic, reviewer;
5. He should be smooth in working and soft talker;
6. He should have good personality traits;
7. He should be well mannered and habitual of reading.

The Reference Function: In many and varied ways reference service will be laid under contribution: in developing the bibliographical sources of the library, in tracking down difficult references, in compiling bibliographies and assembling material, in borrowing on inter-library loan, in securing film and photostats to supplement local materials, and in calling attention to important publications pertinent to research-in-progress. Indeed, the very number of these services and the zeal with which the reference librarian prosecutes them sometimes leads to professional demands upon his time that are wholly unreasonable in view of his other duties.

The service a library can render research is dependent directly on the size of its book funds. If the library is able to purchase all the books needed for instructional purposes and if its collections contain the great and basic books in all fields. There is no use in purchasing specialized indexes and abstract journals unless the library files most of the material indexed. This is a misunderstanding. It is not the library's business to have all the material for actual research, but to be able to trace and borrow it. And this is where printed finding lists and inter-library loan services come in.

14.4 Inter-Library Loans

Inter-library loan service is a recognized function of the reference department because the tools necessary to its proper functioning are found in the reference room collection. It is probable that inter-library loans are even more important in the small library for instructional purposes. They are important in securing for immediate use material whose purchase would involve a delay, as, for example, out-of-print or foreign books. They are important in supplementing the small library's collection of specialized books and journals without which instruction would suffer. It is abundantly evident that no library, not even a great university or research library can possess all the material it needs for research. Because of its limited finances and book resources, the library must look beyond campus boundaries for at least a part of the research materials required by its faculty.

Inter-library loan service was first administered in accord with the American Library Association code. This code stressed the idea that the function of inter-library loan is to serve the research interests of university scholars. It recognizes the loan of books from one library to another as a privilege, not as an obligation. Inter-library loan service has been the foundation stone on which co-operative enterprises have rested. In areas where libraries have established definite programmes for the strengthening of their research resources, a free exchange of materials has been encouraged and practised without difficulty or loss of books. The borrowing library recognize its responsibility in the matter of requesting and making loans. Efforts as necessary as the searching of the card catalogue before ordering new books or the record of the books themselves in the catalogue or the circulation charging trays. These efforts may be summarized under four heads:

1. Locating the most likely source where material may be borrowed. A hit and miss practice of placing requests for loans is all too common. A systematic study of the most likely place where a particular publication may be secured is necessary in making each request for a loan.
2. Verifying the title of the publication requested before borrowing. In all cases, a careful attempt should be made to identify each title to be asked for, and to supply complete bibliographical information so as to prevent unnecessary search at the library to which the request is sent.
3. Substituting photostat and film purchase for inter-library book loans. Whenever possible and practical, the borrowing library should seek to substitute photostatic or film reproductions for the book or journal loan, provided no use is to be made of the material which would in anyway infringe on copyright or right of authorship.
4. *Routine responsibilities*: It is not necessary to outline inter-library loan practices in detail to indicate the major responsibilities in routines. The library, naturally, should assume complete responsibility for transportation costs for observing the rules of the lending library in regard to the use of materials borrowed on inter-library loan, for returning books promptly and safely and in the manner designated by the lending library, and for maintaining the proper

forms and records necessary in requesting, acknowledging, and recording the loans.

The importance of inter-library loan and microfilm and micro-card services in supporting instruction and research having been pointed out, one may properly consider in more detail certain comparatively recent developments in library co-operation. The activities in connection with the programmes of co-operation have taken various forms:

1. *Union catalogues of books and serials*: The former is primarily a university library development but libraries have contributed cards to the central bibliographical center in certain areas. Regional lists of serials have been developed much more extensively and have proved a valuable tool for research purposes.
2. In the acquisition of expensive journals and books not in constant use and used primarily for research purposes, duplication has been avoided by consultation and checking in advance of ordering.
3. Duplication of material has further been avoided by the definition and assignment of specific fields of interest to neighbouring libraries.
4. Through the use of national and regional union lists of serials, individual attempts have been made to build up broken files of journals in one library by the exchange of incomplete sets from other libraries. In this way, one complete file of an important journal is made available to all libraries through inter-library loan.

14.5 Reference Centres

Reference service may provided by (1) a central reference department in a general library building, (2) a central reference department plus several divisional libraries, or (3) decentralized departments either within the central building or in separate departmental libraries.

Many libraries have separate reference and circulation departments, the heads of which report directly to the chief librarian. Larger libraries may place these departments in a division of readers' services, in which he reports to the chief librarian.

Reference services in a public library should start with the collection of Quick Reference books like Directories, Almanacs, Year-books, General Encyclopedias, Atlases, Time tables etc. Supply of standard works, literary, scientific and technical, of a representative character in major subjects should also be provided. Materials on the sources of knowledge — Bibliographies, Indexes etc. should be acquired and if necessary outside assistance should be sought by means of co-operative schemes. Besides, certain specialized services within the library *i.e.* the compilation of indexes to local newspapers, trade names and unexpected sources of information may be performed. Fugitive material, newspaper cuttings and local collection should be properly organized for use.

14.6 Organization

In large libraries the Reference Section can be administratively organized in any of the following ways:

(a) Division by subject, and consolidation of the resources in related subject areas. An organization of materials by broad related subject groups — of library materials, regardless of form, requires fewer separate reading rooms, as all types and forms of materials (books, journals, newspapers, microfilms, etc.) are brought together by subject in one area. Specialized reference services covering all types of materials may be offered in the divisional library.

(b) *Division by form*: In the order departmentalized libraries we find that the materials and services are organized by "form" of publications *e.g.* periodicals, government publications, manuscripts, maps etc. In the principal libraries a functional organization by type or form of library materials may require separate reading rooms for general books, for periodicals etc.

(c) *Subject specialists*: Reference work in a library may also be organized by providing subject specialists. The library materials need not be decentralized by establishing separate collections devoted to particular subjects.

REFERENCES

Authony, L.J., ed. *Handbook of Special Librarianship and Information Work.* London, Aslib, 1982.

Fanton, D.M. "Reference Librarian." *Jrl. of Higher Edu.* 9; 153-56.

Grogan, Devis. *Practical Reference Work.* London, Clive Bingley, 1979.

McKel, Bob. *Planning Library Service.* London, Clive Bingley, 1989.

Sadler, Philip. *Managing Change.* London, Kegan Press, 1995.

Sharma, C.D. *Advances in Library and Information Science.* Jaipur, Scientific Publishers, 1992.

Sharma, C.K. *Sandarva Sewa.* Delhi, Metropolitan, 1977.

Sharma, C.K. *Granthalaya Main Sandharva Sewa.* Aligarh, Jagrati, 1991.

Thomas, D.M. *The Effective Reference Librarian.* New York, Acad. Press, 1981.

15

Inter-library Loan

15.1 Introduction

Inter-library loan is a media of library co-operation. It can be achieved on the three levels of library activities. It may be within the library; among libraries and libraries of other cities, states and countries.

Inter-library loan is a temporary loan which takes place for specific period of time. Ranganathan's fifth law implies that library is a growing organism and every part and the particles of the library should flow constantly. A large number of books are published every year and it has become difficult rather impossible to collect and preserve all the books in a single library. Every library selects the books to meet its own needs. Even the highest library can never hope, and usually never intends, to have everything which its clientele may desire. Every library has its limitation of size, stock and the finance which compel the library to expend upto a certain limit. On the other hand a library is supposed to provide maximum service to the readers through its various resources; but no library can be independent and has to depend on the various libraries for meeting the different needs of the readers. The alternative to this is Intern-library loan. This implies that each library remain dependent upon each other fulfilling the needs of the clientele. This can be achieved only if books of a library can be issued to the members of the other libraries. The libraries can establish and maintain an adequate service to research scholars only by encouraging schemes of co-operation between themselves locally, regionally and nationally. Inter-library loan is most important of all the types of co-operative activities.

Inter-library loan system as first suggested in American by S.S. Green in 1876 and Rechardon in 1905. There were several factors which extended the inter-library loan activities *i.e.* the increase in amount of research and the students and the faculty members in universities. In 1892 Melvil Dewey advised the librarians to make proper use of Inter-library loan. Lane suggested to form central storage houses and bureau of information, which may serve as inter-library loan centres to all libraries. There are other basic needs like safety in transportation, indemnity of losses, preparing union lists and sufficient finance which makes the system effective. According to a survey of university libraries Carl M. White pointed out that "...the value of these longer efforts and services, however, must, if there are to be understood all, be measured in terms of economy of time and money and in meeting urgent needs of the learned world".

Small libraries depend on big libraries. Some libraries have a pressure of work of inter-library loan as they are the only libraries in the region. Bigger library provides material, copies of material, to users in all parts of the country.

A.L.A. has introduced a inter-library loan code 1904. It stressed on the following points that:

(i) it should serve the graduates and the researchers of universities, and

(ii) it should be recognized as a privilege, not as an obligation.

Some libraries have the old pattern to conduct the inter-library loan activities. They have unwritten codes of conduct which were rather loose. A.L.A. code has given a systematized method of inter-library loan which includes the purpose, scope, material not applied for, material to be sent, limit of number of volume, duration of loan, safeguards, general provisions and suggestions, responsibility of borrowers and notices of receipt and return. Library collects various type of material, rare, general and reference. Rare material should not be loaned out in the event of their lost, as they cannot be replaced.

U.K. started inter-library loan method in 1916 when National Central Library began functioning to students. Kenuen

Committee on public libraries recommended for central clearing house of inter-library loan network. The other effort was made by Perry Committee which suggested the inter-lending library scheme for England and Wales. Waledage and Page took large idea and suggested that the National Central Library should work as the "(inter-library) intermediary in the important service of loans between British and foreign libraries."

In India the system of inter-library loan has becoming popular day by day. The first effort was made by National Library, Calcutta in 1903 when it made necessary agreement with the Asiatic Society of Bengal. National Library has developed a separate inter-library loan division. Moreover, it has reached to an agreement with Library of Congress, Washington and the National Central Library, London, which has given fruitful result in the field of research. University libraries in India, loan books to each other on reciprocal basis. INSDOC also serve the scientists through inter-library loan scheme and borrow books or periodicals from other Indian libraries on loan.

15.2 Categories of Books

Ranganathan has categorized the books to be loaned by the libraries in two divisions. He has made this division with the idea of providing more reading facilities to the local clientele.

1. *Prohibited categories*:
   - (a) Books costing less than 10 rupees unless they are technical or special publications or they are more than five years old;
   - (b) Textbooks or quasi textbooks, required continuously for examination purposes;
   - (c) Fiction and quick reference books;
   - (d) Books for which the indenting library has a copy; and
   - (e) Loose numbers of periodicals.
2. *Right of the lending library*:
   - (a) Loan of a book may be deferred;
   - (b) In the recent additions, to such time as the local demand may be justified;

(c) In case of a book for which there is an unusual temporary demand, to such time as may be necessary;

(d) Loan of a book may be subjected to special conditions;

(e) The loan of any book may be refused without assigning any reason.

In some countries it is customary for the national library and a designated university library to serve as sole agencies for international inter-library loan and copying services.

Inter-library loan system between the local and regional library can secure the co-ordination of purchase and specialization in subject. Ranganathan has suggested some rules for inter-library loan in the report of U.G.C. Committee for university and college libraries. The U.G.C. report again discussed the importance of union catalogue and its preparation. In its opinion, it is very difficult to prepare a union catalogue of the whole material. It should be confined to material of research value such as (i) learned periodicals, (ii) books in out of the way language, (iii) costly concerned treatises, and (iv) rare books.

Inter-library loan service involves an expenditure up to a certain limit. Libraries charge the cost of postage and the security of the material called under inter-library loan. "The cost of inter-library loan very considerably depending on how they are handled out whether or not that are completed". The collection of fees for inter-library loan varies from library to library. In many libraries transportation charges are taken in full; while others charge only a flat fee. Inter-library loan varies from library to library. In many university libraries transportation charges are taken in full. Inter-library loan service is a courtesy and privilege and thus the libraries find it difficult to appropriate the expenditure.

In Indian universities, a flat fee is charged which differs from one library to the other. A sum of Rs. 10 is being charged by the cost of the libraries as inter-library loan fee to meet the to and fro postal or transport charges. The fee collected in university libraries range between Rs. 10 to Rs. 20. Ranganathan recommended a free library service and described inter-library loan service, an obligation of the university library itself. In his opinion the borrowing library is to pay to and fro transport and other incidental charges.

UGC sub-committee of U.K. has recommended —

1. A lending scheme should be as sufficient and speedy as possible but carefully regulated and controlled in view of the cost.

2. If delay in meeting a loan request is directly due to short of staff in a university library, the university has a duty to provide such staff.

15.3 Loan Application Form

A.L.A. code for inter-library loan has suggested a simple inter-library loan request form as per given on next page. Jacques worked on a UNESCO project for standardization of inter-library loan request form and also suggested the form shown as under:

INTER-LIBRARY LOAN REQUEST FORM

Inter-library form request		Request A
(According to the ALA inter-library loan code)		
		REPORTS: Checked by......
Date of requests: (Borrowing library, Full in left half of form: send sheets A, B and C to lending library and enclose shipping level).	Remark:	sent by: Bookrate exp. collected insured for \$ Date sent.......changes........ Date due........................ (for period of loan) For use in library only.
For use of...status...Deptt. Author (or periodical title, Vol. & year)		NOT SENT BECAUSE: Not owned-by library. Non-circulating
Call No. Title (either author and Pages for periodical articles) (incl. Edition, place and date verified in or source of reference)		Hold placed In use Request again Other Suggest your request of......
Lending: If non-consulting, please sent Library: sent estimate for......		REQUEST: (Borrowing library fill in)

Inter-library form request	Request A
Microprints Microfilms Authorized by:	Date vol. Received............ Date vol. Returned .... By Book rate Expenses prepaid Others Insured for RENEWALS Requested on: Renewed to: (or period of renewal)

BOOK EXCHANGE REQUEST FORM

(Front side)

A. Request for exchange publication		
To:	From:	Date of request
Author:		
Title:		
Publisher (Place, date):		
Reference:		
Remarks:		
To be returned with reply (P.T.O.)		

(Back side)

B. To be returned with reply	checked.	Date of reply:
1. Enclosed		
2. Sent separately		
3. Not yet published: will be sent later (probably in.......)		
4. Not yet published: request later.		
5. Can be sent in microfilm. May be purchased from........		
6. Not available by exchange. May be purchased from......		
7. Already sent.		
8. Not published in our country, by our institution		
9. Out of print		
10. Stopped after v. n. year.		
11. Cannot identify, more detail please.		
12. Other answers		

REFERENCES

Indwar, R.P. "Inter-library Co-operation in India." *ILA Bull.* 2, 1966.

Kapoor, S.B.P. "Inter-Library Co-operation in India." *ILA Bull.* 2, 1966.

Melinev, C.H. "Inter-Library Lending." *Lib. Trg.* 2, 1954.

Patil, P.K. "Inter-Library Co-operation." *ILA Bull.* 2, 1966.

Richardson, E.C. "Co-operation in Lending among College & Reference Libraries." *Lib. Jrl.* 29, 1991.

Sehgal, S.M. "Inter Lib. Co-op. in India." *ILA Bull.* 2, 1966.

Trivedi, N.L. "Inter-Library Co-op. in Scientific & Tech. Libraries." *Ind. Libn.* 22, 1967.

16

ANNUAL REPORT

An Annual Report is a survey of the actual work done during the preceding year. It differs from a budget as the latter is an estimate for the covering year while the former is the medium through which we can know the progress or regress of various departments during the previous year.

It differs from the Annual Financial Statement in that the latter restricts itself to financial aspects only whereas the former covers all aspects including financial matters.

Now-a-days every department has to —

(a) report about its working,

(b) report to the superior authority,

(c) report annually or the demanded,

(d) report to aware of the achievements and shortcomings of the respective departments.

The report is customary with commercial companies to prepare periodical sheets.

The report includes —

(a) actual condition

(b) financial position

(c) services

(d) assets

(e) liabilities

(f) public utility position

16.1 Purpose

1. It is a written document.

2. It is to present the actual position to the authorities.
3. To know the actual financial position.
4. To review the readers demand.
5. To review the physical need/reading material.
6. To covers the patterns about the services.
7. To highlight the achievements
8. To highlight the shortcomings.
9. To make further planning for development.
10. To highlights the hindrances and bottlenecks in order to revere them in future.
11. To highlight the financial conditions of library.
12. To know the actual need of the library.
13. To judge the efficiency of the librarian and the staff.
14. To judge the application of the library standards.

16.2 Special Features of Annual Report

1. Form of Report

(a) Report should be presented in each format to enable a layman to understand.

(b) Report should be presented in tables, graphs and narrated fashion.

(c) Easy catchwords should be used to be disseminate clearly to the notice of the readers.

2. Contents of the Report

Contents is an important feature. It can be divided in following parts while preparing report:

1. The clientele
2. Book stock
3. The technical services
4. Public services
5. Finances
6. Miscellaneous

1. *Clientele* is a main stay of a library. It indicates —

(a) Popularity of a library.

(b) Actual and potential readership.

(c) To understand and to think the ways and means to bring down the gap between the actual and potential readership.

(d) Clientele is to judge the usefulness of a library.

2. *The Book Stock*

Books stock is an essential part of the library. The report may clarify —

(a) The collection of the book stock.

(b) The field of specialization.

(c) The additions of book stock in the year.

(d) The withdrawal of book stock in the year.

(e) Broader subject matter.

(f) The number of current periodicals.

(g) The back volumes of the periodicals.

3. *Technical Services*

Technical services are backbone of a library. Technical services provides —

(a) Necessity of services.

(b) The order of services, and their use by readers.

(c) Scheme of classification.

(d) Cataloguing system.

(e) Documentation work/services.

(f) Impact of technical services on library services.

(g) Staff technicality for the services.

(h) Adequacy of technical services in accordance with the accepted norms.

4. *Public Services*

There are services rendered to the readers directly. These consists of —

(a) The provision of facilities for borrowing books.

(b) Modes of public services — mobile or by post.

(c) Advisory services.

(d) Reference services.

(e) Indexing services, abstracting services.

(f) Documentation services.

(g) Latest devices used or to be used.

5. *Reference*

Finance is the crux of the problem. Financial need is evident. The report should include —

(a) Actual financial conditions:

  (i) Income itemwise

  (ii) Expenditure itemwise

(b) Budget allocation

(c) Standards and norms of expenditure

(d) Average percentage of expenditure

(e) Sources of revenue:

  (i) Recurring

  (ii) Non-recurring

(f) Future plan to enhance sources.

6. *Miscellaneous Activities*

(a) Lectures

(b) Film shows

(c) Social and adult education activities

(d) Inter-library co-operation.

16.3 Draft of Annual Report

Year.............

A. General

1. Name of the library ....
2. Nature of the library ....
3. Date of Establishment ....
4. Area/population served .... Rural/Urban.......
5. Working hours
6. No. of days closed in a year

B. Clientele

1. Total number of members
2. Male

3. Female
4. Children
5. Total no. of active members
6. New members added during the period ....
7. Conditions of membership
8. Ratio of members to the total population ....

C. Book Stock

	Books	*Periodicals*	*Others*
1. Total no. of volumes of the beginning of the year			
2. Number of volumes added during the year			
3. No. of volumes withdrawn during the year			
4. Total no. of volumes at the close of the year			
5. Total no. of current periodicals subscribed			
6. Total no. of volumes in stock per head of population			

D. Technical Services

1. Whether the book stock is classified or not.
2. Classification scheme in use... Dewey/Colon etc.
3. Catalogue scheme in use Dictionary/classified etc.
4. Physical form of the catalogue:
   (i) Card/Book/Sheaf
   (ii) MSS/typed/printed

E. Staff

1. Total number of employees
2. Professional
3. Semi-professional
4. Unskilled

F. Public Services

I. 1. Issue system in vogue : Newark/Browns/others

2. Total number of books issued and returned during the year ....

3. Average number of books issued daily.

4. No. of books issued according to the subject Fiction .... Non-fiction ....Biography.........

II. Reference Service:

1. Total no. of reference vols. in stock .... General .... specific subject ....

2. No. of books consulted daily ....

3. No. of enquiries received daily ....

4. Total no. of readers who used the reference section during the period.

5. Types of enquiries received for answering:

(a) Fact finding

(b) Directories

(c) Research type

III. Indexing, abstracting & documentation:

1. No. of indexes made ....

2. No. of indexes used ....

3. No. of periodical articles abstracted ....

4. No. of periodicals articles documented ....

IV. Mobile Library services:

1. No. of villages/deposit centres/stations visited...

2. No. of average working hours per week.

3. No. of books issued and returned during the period.

G. Finance

1. Expenditure: *Budget* *Actual*

(a) Recurring:

(i) Books and back sets

(ii) Current periodicals

(iii) Staff Salary

(iv) Wages

(v) Binding

(vi) Building repair

(vii) Heating and cooling charges

(viii) Postage, telephones

(ix) Stationery & equipments

(x) Mobile Vans

(xi) Spl. Grant for books

(xii) Other services

(b) Non-recurring

(c) Total

2. Revenue:

(a) Library rate

(b) State Government grant

(c) Endowments

(d) Others

Total Surplus Deficit

H. Cost Accounting

1. Cost of service per book ....
2. Cost of service per reader ....
3. Budget provision per reader/per capita.

I. Miscellaneous

1. General conditions of the library ....
2. New services rendered
3. Extra mural activities
4. Inter-library co-operation
5. Publications, if any
6. Any other suggestions.

Dated..........

Signature of the Librarian/
Chairman of Library Committee

16.4 Compilation of Annual Report

Annual report is compiled by the librarian with the help of Dy./Asstt. Librarian and section in-charges. Librarian collect the datas and edits it.

The period of report may be either the calendar year or the financial year. Generally it is financial year being the budget year.

The following procedures is adopted to prepare the annual report —

1. It is given final shape before or in the first week of the reporting year.
2. It is finally approved by the librarian in the last month of the reporting year.
3. The copies of proforma are sent to each of the section in-charge for collecting the necessary information.
4. Each section fill up the proforma relating to his section along with the statements of the information in support of the information given in the proforma.
5. Each section return the proforma within the 2nd week of the last month.
6. All the data are checked and verified by the Dy. Librarian. In case of discrepancy, it is returned to section to revise it.
7. The draft Annual Report is prepared by the Dy. Librarian on the basis of the data received by him.
8. Dy. Librarian consult the last year report and prepare the average ratio of the increase or decrease of the achieved data in comparison with the previous year.
9. Data is prepared in tabular form about the services performed by each section of the library.
10. An introduction, summarise the salient features of the year is prepared.
11. The final draft annual report is presented to the librarian for his approval.
12. The librarian, if suggest any change, it is incorporated in it.

13. The draft is finally prepared.
14. The draft is typed and multiple copies are prepared after the signature of librarian.
15. Two copies of the report are submitted to library authority/board/highest body for information and review.
16. After the report is reviewed by the library authority action is taken accordingly.

REFERENCES

Danton, J.P. *Dimensions of Comparative Librarianship.* Chicago, ALA, 1973.

Gates, J.K. *Introduction to Librarianship.* New York, McGraw Hill, 1968.

Oldman, C.M. *Value of Information.* Bradford, Management Consult., 1976.

Pratt, A.D. "*Analysis of Library Statistics.*" *Lib. Qrly.* 45, 1975.

Ranganathan, S.R. *Five Laws of Lib. Science.* Bombay, Asia, 1957.

Rawski, C.H. *Towards a Theory of Librarianship.* N. Jersey, Scarecrow, 1973.

Reed, S.R. "Evaluation of Library Services." *Lib. Trends.* 22, 1974.

Tauber, M.F. *Library Surveys.* New York, Columbia Univ. Press, 1967.

17

BUDGET

Natchez and Bupp

The budget reflects simultaneously a yearly process of administration and decisions among alternative political priorities. Budgets are at once measures of the way Government is organized and of the policy decisions the organization implements.

17.1 Importance

Budget consists of following points —

1. It summarise categories of expenditure.
2. It transmits budget information.
3. It is coded statement.
4. It clarifies the individual expenditure.
5. It is an object of the library and organization.
6. It is a process of smooth working of the library.
7. It limits the role of all individuals.
8. It controls the succeeding year's activities.

17.2 Aspects

Budget has three aspects —

1. Planning
2. Management
3. Control

1. Planning

(a) Planning is clearly associated with preparation of budget.

(b) Planning reflects continuous process which is prepared on the basis of budget.

(c) Objections of an institution are assessed, reviewed and restated.

2. Management

(a) It is a process by which necessary resources are obtained in order to achieve:

(i) Objectives

(ii) Safeguards against reasonable expenditure.

(b) It guards librarian against possible change.

(c) It prevent clash.

(d) It curbs the exercise of discretionary powers.

3. Control

It is a process by which adherence of policy is ensured.

17.3 Why Budgetary Control

1. A budget is simply a planning document. It is prepared in summary form of categories and amount of expenditure.
2. Price increase is uneven and likely to be covered in expenditure.
3. Simple budget, simple administration.
4. Library statistics are not enough for the budget for casting.
5. Influence on external influences must be considered in budget.
6. Administrator must rely on information of subordinate officers.
7. Administrator should very well know the policies and procedures decided by the governing body.
8. Debates should be organized to discuss the budget.
9. Administrator should know the rigidity and saving devices so that rigidity may be minimised and saving may be increased.
10. Budget reflects policies. Hence policies are decided in light of financial programme.

11. Budget should be prepared by standard procedures.
12. There should be decentralized control of budget. But some funds should be centrally governed such as — staff salary and other facilities.

17.4 Sources of Finance

1. Funds allotted by the institution
2. Funds allotted by the government
3. Funds received by donation
4. Funds received through subscription fee
5. Funds received through sale of publications
6. Library cess
7. Library fines
8. Financial organization
9. Library discount.

1. Funds allotted by the institution

Every institution or the authority of the library allot some budget to its library out of his total budget. In case of public libraries, it is government or the local government and its library committee. In case of Academic library, it is the University, Institution or the Management of the schools. In case of special libraries, the controlling authority or the institute to which the library belongs. The funds vary from library to library on the basis of the nature of the library.

2. Funds allotted by the government

Government also provides necessary funds through library grant to public libraries, academic libraries and special libraries. This grant is of types — Recurring grant to public libraries and school libraries and Non-recurring grant to University, College and special libraries.

3. Funds received by donation

Donations are also received by libraries. These donations are by public, and organizations without any condition. The conditional donation is not received by the libraries. Donation of books are also treated as financial support to the libraries.

4. Funds received through subscription fee

In European countries subscription is an important source of finance as there libraries are generally subscription libraries.

In India it is not practiced except American and British Council libraries. There are few other but not popular.

On the whole libraries charge library fee for membership which is not refundable. It is other than caution money.

However, such library fee is an important source of finance.

5. Funds received through sale of publications

There are libraries which are published special books like indexes, abstracts, bibliographies. These are priced publications and sold by libraries. Moreover, few libraries publish journals which accrues the income. All such revenue is the financial source of libraries.

6. Library cess

Library cess is levied in some states directly or by enactment of Library Legislation like Tamil Nadu, Andhra Pradesh, Karnataka etc. There is a provision of library cess in most of the Library Acts except in West Bengal, Haryana and Maharashtra.

Library cess is levied at different rates in different states, ranges from paise 8 per rupee on House and Property tax and fully spent on Public libraries of the state. Central Govt. has no library legislation and no library cess.

7. Library fines

Majority of the libraries charge overdue fines and the rate ranging from 25 paise per day to Rs. 10 per day. It collects a heavy amount and utilized in library. It is treated as source of income of library.

8. Financial organization

There are institutions and councils/commissions meant by the government to sanction financial help to various types of libraries *e.g.*:

(a) University Grant Commission — To Universities and Colleges.

(b) ICAR, ICMR, ICHR, ICSSR — To Universities, Colleges and special libraries.

(c) Raja Ram Mohan Roy Foundation — To social

institutions, schools and for adult education programme by libraries.

(d) Literacy House, like for libraries of rural areas.

9. Library discount

Though library discount, allowed by the publishers on purchasing of books @ Rs. 10% to 20% is a sort of source of income. It is not a direct source of income, but indirectly it effect the library budget.

17.5 Preparation of Budget

1. Duration of budget
2. Section-wise budget — Financial requirements of the sections.
3. Record should be based on objects
4. Last year expenditure
5. Current expenditure
6. Estimated expenditure for next year
7. Standard norms

17.6 Budget Allocation

Usual budget items

Receipts	*Expenditure*
1. Last year balance	1. Salary staff
2. Library cess	2. Books
3. Govt. grant	3. Periodicals
4. Donation/Gift	4. Building
5. Fines	5. Audio-visual
6. Other sources	6. Rent
7. Permanent/Recurring Grant	7. Heat/light/water
	8. Stationery/telephone
	9. Printing
	10. Insurance
	11. Maintenance
	12. Miscellaneous

INDIA

1. University Library/College Library

Books	25%
Periodicals	35%
Staff	30%
Buildings & other	20%

2. Public Library

Books	35%
Periodicals	25%
Staff	30%
Buildings & other	20%

UK Medium Size Library

Books	53%
Periodicals	21%
Building	15%
Salary	10%

U.K. University Library

Salary	50%
Books	25%
Periodicals	15%
Building	5%
Sundries	5%

USA Education Statistics

8 Categories — Salaries, staff, wages, books, periodicals, binding, audio-visual material, maintenance.

SCONUL Financial Report USA

Staff	50%
Book grant	50%

University Library

Books	25%
Periodicals	40%
Binding	20% of book grant
Sundries	10%
Staff	25%

REFERENCES

Allen, K.S. *Current and Emerging Budgeting Techniques in Academic Libraries.* Washington, Seattle, 1972.

Barner, Frank. *Budget Priorities for Libraries.* Mebowewe, Ormoud, 1971.

Cutt, James. *A Planning, Programming and Budget Manual.* New York, Praeger, 1974.

Ells Worth, Ralph E. "Some Aspects of the Problem of Allocating Book Funds for University Libraries." *Lib. Qrly.* 2; 488-89.

Gopinath, M.A. "Financial Norms for Collection Development in Libraries." *Lib. Sc.* 20, 1983.

Mason, D. "Programmed Budgeting and Cost Effectiveness." *Aslib Procgs.* 25, 1973.

Mc Gum. "Ground Work in Budget Making." *ALA Bull.* 29; 132-33.

Muller, Hans. "The Management of College Lib. Funds...." *Coll. & Res. Lib.* 2; 32.

Orr, R.H. "Measuring the Goodness of Lib. Service." *Jrl. of Doc.* 29, 1973.

Rohef, R.H. *Library Cast and Budget.* Minnesota Libraries 24; 39-45.

Sharma, C.K. *University Library: Management & Organization.* Delhi, Metropolitan, 1977.

Williams, S.F. "To Charge or Not to Charge." *Ref. Libn.* 19, 1987.

18

LIBRARY STATISTICS

Statistics are tabulated figures which are employed by most of the modern sciences in order to gauge the progress or regress in various fields of study.

Statistics are 'facts in figures'.

The descriptive details are reduced to figures so that the important facts are brought to the notice of the public in a readable and intelligible manner.

Statistical bringout the facts in an objective or unbiased manner. Statistics are instrumental in gauging the progress or regress of the library at a given time if the figures of the past are compared with those of the present.

The statistics should be used with due care caution and all the factors which count or effect must be taken into consideration at the time of comparison.

18.1 Method of Presentation

Statistics can be presented in —

(a) Tables

(b) Graphs

(c) Maps

(d) Other diagrammatic form in proper method of recording the fluctuating facts.

Statistics indicate clearly and concisely the results obtained —

1. Tabulated foım should be simple and clear.
2. Diagrams and graphs should be devised as to the facts and the truth.

3. Different kinds of figures should be written in different colours and sizes.
4. The most symbolic and appealing method of presentation of statistical should be used.

18.2 Utility of Library Statistics

1. It is fundamental instrument in planning and control.
2. It is a recognized method of providing an adequate check on current performance.
3. It is a basis for long range planning.
4. Statistics are quantitative in nature.
5. It present the overall picture of the library.
6. The scientific handling of statistics eliminate play of vague feelings and reduce the chances for unreliable conclusions.
7. It will bring to the surface and reveal tendencies and factors.
8. It will furnish correct conclusions.
9. It will furnish quantitative conclusions.
10. It will furnish reliable conclusions.
11. Statistics are the best bases for the preparation of an Annual Report.

18.3 Sources of Library Statistics

1. Register by every section.
2. Diary by every section.
3. Annual report.
4. Display methods/Display board.
5. Publicity methods (Newspaper, Bulletin, Annual magazine of the organization).

Kinds of statistics

We can divide statistics into three classes —

1. Statistics of Technical Department.
2. Statistics of Service Department.
3. Miscellaneous Statistics.

18.4 Technical Services

The technical work is known as 'work behind the screen' such as —

(a) Demanding the book-lists.

(b) Preparing the orders.

(c) Receiving the books.

(d) Processing the books —

(i) Accessioning

(ii) Classifying

(iii) Cataloguing

(e) Work load on staff members in technical section.

Work in Technical Section

1. Classification

Month..............Year...........

Sl. No.	Name of the incumbent and Designation	No. of Books classified............... Days of the month.
		1 2 3 4 5 6 7 8 9 10 11 12 13 14 15.... Total
1.	Shri.......... Classifier	
2.	Shri........... Classifier	

2. Cataloguing

Month..............Year............

No. of books catalogued and No. of cards prepared........

Sl. No.	Name of the incumbent and Designation	No. of Books classified.................. Days of the month.
		1 2 3 4 5 6 7 8 9 10 11 12 13 14 15.... Total
3.	Shri.......... Classifier	
4.	Shri.......... Classifier	

3. Acquisition Section

It is essential to know the name of —

(a) books,

(b) pamphlets,

(c) other reading material

Month________________ Year________________

Reading material	000	100	200	300	400	500	Total
By Purchase:							
Books							
Pamphlets							
Others							
Total							
By Exchange:							
Books							
Pamphlets							
Others							
Total							
By Gift:							
Books							
Pamphlets							
Others							
Total							

4. Periodical Section

Month________________ Year____________

Frequency of Publication	No. of Periodicals	No. of Periodicals	No. of reminder	No. of reminder
Daily				
Weekly				
Fortnightly				
Others				
Total				

5. 1. *Indexing, Abstracting and Documentation Services*

Week No.________ Month____________ Year________

Subject	No. of periodicals indexed	No. of articles abstracted	No. of articles reproduced
000			
100			
200			
300			
400			
500			
600			
700			
800			
900			
Total			

Service Departments

Date	Sl. No.	Name and address of	Occupation Class	Sex	Age Group	Sign

2. *Daily Attendance Statistics*

Date	No. of readers who visited the company	Occupation of class	Sex	Age Group

3. *Issue Statistics*

Date	Subjects	No. of Books Issued	No. of books returned	No. of books renewed	No. of books lost
	Poetry				
	Drama				
	Novel				
	Short stories				
	Other literature				
	Biographies				
	Useful Art				
	History and travels				
	Other non-fiction				
	Total				

4. *Issue Statistics Languagewise*

Date	Language	No. of books issued
	English	
	Hindi	
	Punjabi	
	Urdu	
	South Language	
	Bengali	
	Oriya	
	Others	

5. ***Issue Statistics Readerwise***

Date	Name of Readers	No. of books issued
	Adults	
	Male	
	Female	
	Children	
	Blind	
	Sick	
	Other abnormals	
	Total	

6. ***Membership Statistics***

Date	No. of Members enrolled	No. of withdrawing members	Total No. of members	Total No. of Actual members

7. ***Classified Issue Register***

Date	Subjects	No. of Books issued
	100	
	200	
	300	
	400	
	500	
	600	
	700	
	800	
	900	
	Total	

8. Classwise Issue Register

Date	Class	No. of books issued
	Higher Secondary	
	Graduate	
	Post-Graduate	
	Teachers	
	Research Scholars	
	Total	

9. ***Issue Statistical Material-wise***

Date_________ No. of Vols. issued_________

Name of Material	331	332	333	334	335	336	337	338	339	Total
Books										
Pamphlets										
Other material										
Total										

1. *Reference department*

In case of closed access, we can prepare the statistics —

Books consulted

Date	No. of books consulted									
000	100	200	300	400	500	600	700	800	900	Total

2. *Reference querries*

Date_______________ Month____________ Year _____

No. of Readers directed	No. of short range enquiries answered	No. of long range enquiries answered	No. of enquiries unanswered	Total

3. *Income and Expenditure*

Item	Book fund	Periodical fund	Staff fund	Others	Total
Income					
Expenditure					

4. *Staff Statistics*

Month__________ Year__________

Name of Post	No. of posts filled	No. of posts lying vacant	Amount spent on salaries	Amount saved on staff salaries

5. *Stock verification statistics*

Sl. No.	Total Collection	Books missing			Total
		Cost Realized	Missing	Books defaced	
Books					
Other material					

REFERENCES

Barness, R.M. *Nation and Time Study.* New York, Wiley, 1968.

Busha, C.M. *Research Methods in Librarianship.* New York, Academic Press, 1980.

"College and University Lib. Statistics." *Call. & Res. Lib.* 9, 245

Gulchrist, A. "Work Study in Libraries." *Jrl. of Libnship.* 2, 1970.

Hare, G. "Performance Measurement." *Inf. & Lib. Manager* 8, 1989.

Hirsch, F.E. "Standards for Libraries." *Lib. Trends* 21, 1972.

Hines, T.C. "Evaluation of Processing Services." *Lib. Trends* 22, 1974.

Jones, Arthner. "Criteria for the Evaluation of Public Library Services." *Jrl. of Libnship.* 2, 1970.

Mallaber, K.A. *International Standardisation of Lib. Statistics.* Hague, IFLA, 1968.

Mann, P. "Public Library Statistics, A Trend Analysis." *J. Lib. Admn.* 14, 1, 1991.

Mcclure, C.R. "Planning Process: Strategies for Action." *Coll & Res. Libraries* 39, 1978.

Orr, R.H. "Measuring the Goodness of Library Services." *Jrl. of Doc.* 29, 1973.

Pennathrr, K. *Work Study for Management.* New Delhi, Popams, 1969.

Pratt, A.D. "An Analysis of Library Statistics." *Lib. Qrly.* 45, 1975.

Schriher, T.J. *Fundamentals of Flow Charting.* Melbourne, Krieger, 1981.

Sariya, M. "Productivity Measurement in Acad. Libraries."

Taylor, J.C. *Survey of Organization, a Machine Scored Standardized Questionnaire Instrument.* Michigan University, 1972.

Thomas, P.A. *Task Analysis of Library Operations.* London, Aslib, 1971.

Urguburt, J.A. "Measuring Readers Failure at the Shelf." *Jrl. of Doc.* 27, 1971.

Wessd, C.J. *Criteria for Evaluating the Effectiveness of Lib. Operations and Services.* Phase-II: Data Gathering. Washington, Thompson, 1967.

Woodruff, Elaire. "Work Measurement Applied to Libraries." *Spl. Lib.* 48, 1957.

19

LIBRARY ROUTINE WORK AND RECORD

Library has to maintain many records in its routine work other than Annual report and Annual budget. There are various activities done by the library in its various sections. The record is to judge the working of a library and make it easy and precise. Record is maintained for essential services and put up before the authorities as and when required.

Definition: In order to describe the performance and measures the success of his organisation, it is necessary for the librarian to have available significant and complete records of sources.

Such record help to show —

1. Accomplishment of the record,
2. Cost of its services,
3. The shortcomings in its organization.

The word 'Record' means "to write something in such a manner that it is available in a permanent form and that it has a lasting value". Record provides —

1. Authoritative information,
2. Authentic information,
3. Factual information.

Record contain the original information whereas statistics can be distorted in a derived direction though based on records.

19.1 Importance

1. It can facilitate the work of the library committee.

2. It is based for deciding the volume of financial assistance.
3. It clarify the activities before the authorities whether library has been properly utilized or not.
4. Tax-payer can be satisfied only through factual records.
5. Records reveals the previous history.
6. Records justify the objectives of a library.

Kind of Records

Records are maintained about books, and equipments, the readers and services. These may be better classified as —

1. Records of books and other non-book resources available in the library.
2. Cost records *i.e.* total cost and unit cost, etc.
3. Service records *i.e.* services rendered by the library;
4. Administrative record.

19.2 Record of Books

Books are for use and every reader is to avail the facilities to read the books. Books are purchased out of public funds. It is essential to justify each penny. Auditors are to be satisfied regarding expenditure as they come as checks and balances against the executive action. It is possible when office maintain every/all records properly.

Example —

If any reader damages or losses the books of the library, library record show help in ascertaining the actual cost price of the lost book, which is to be realized from the defaulter reader or replace the book. For this purpose the *Accession Register* is maintained.

The following record is maintained regarding the books —

1. Order book,
2. Accession Register,
3. Book selection cards
4. Bill Entry register
5. Bill payment register
6. Budget allocation register (subject allocation).

Record of Non-book Material

For non-book material *i.e.* films, microfilms, micro cards, maps, atlases, gramophone records, cassettes, C.D., Floppy etc. this type of material is maintained by keeping records like —

1. Accession register.
2. Subject-wise category register.
3. Register by type of material.

Account Record

1. Allocation Register

   Name of Deptt./Subject...... Total amount sanctioned

   Name of the Head of grant

Sl. No.	Bill No. Date	Name of the Supplier	Amount of the bill	Deduction if any	Total of the bill	Total grant of the Deptt.	Remarks

2. Bill Register

Sl. No.	Date of passing for payment	Bill No. Date	Name of the Supplier	Amount of the bill	Deptt. to which debited	Total grant	Balance

3. Bill files
4. Shelf-list
5. Book catalogue
6. Technical record:
   (a) Staff manual
   (b) Classi. & cataloguing procedures.

7. Cost record:
   (a) Sale and wage register
   (b) Library building register
   (c) Building maintenance register
   (d) Maintenance register (Electric, cooling, postage, and telephone)
   (e) Miscellaneous (stationery).
8. Service Record:
   (a) Visitors record/register

Date	Sl. No.	Name of Visitor	Address	Occupation	Purpose of Visit	Remarks

   (b) Issue records
      (i) Readers Record (Registration)
      (ii) Time Record (borrowing period)
      (iii) Overdue records
      (iv) Reserved book record.
9. Reference Department:
   Reference librarian maintains the following records —
   (a) Reference diary
   (b) Visitors of Ref. Deptt.'s register
   (c) Register for nature of enquiries — sport range/ Language.
10. Administration records:
   (a) Daily attendance register
   (b) Duties allocation chart
   (c) Casual leave register
   (d) Privilege leave register
   (e) Salary register
   (f) Gradation of staff register

(g) Contingency register

(h) Cash security deposits register.

11. Record Section:

(a) Register for record-register

(b) Register of files.

20

Preservation of Library Material

The library stand for collection of books.

The word 'conservation' originates which means 'to keep', 'to preserve': It means —

1. To preserve from destructive influence.
2. Natural decay or waste.
3. Preservation in being, health and perfection.

The process of conservation may be divided into two parts —

1. Preservation in which attempts are made to resist or delay the deteriorating effects of the environment and like, and
2. Restoration in which action are taken to improve physical condition, so that the effects of the deterioration can be entirely or partially removed and its original or near original condition restored.

Protecting consciously any material from being damaged by conditions both internal and external through deterioration as an effect of situations prevailing in the environment, conditions invaded in the materials or due to sudden natural calamity or accidents etc., is known as 'Preservation'.

Books are the life blood of great thinkers of the past and the present. It is a very pleasant, though difficult task of a librarian to preserve the treasure of knowledge which is found in the form of books and documents. It is rather his religious duty to conserve this knowledge in an appropriate manner.

Books like human being have got a body and soul —

Body – Material of which the book is made, paper, ink, binding.

Soul – Actual thought content found in written pages of the book.

Librarian has two fold obligations —

1. Preserving the book.
2. Publicizing the book.

20.1 Physical Constituents or Main Components of a Book

There are following constituents of a book —

1. Paper
2. Ink
3. Leather/Rexin/Cloth
4. Thread
5. Adhesives

Generally paper is manufactured from rags, wood, cotton, bamboo, grass, straw etc. There are many mechanical processes — pulping process, cutting machines to cut the cellulose fibres *e.g.* rag, cotton, jute. They are collected and divided in groups according to their nature, colour etc. The further process is —

(a) Put in alkaline water in a big vat.

(b) It is boiled.

(c) Bleacher is used to bleach to destroy unwanted colour.

(d) Pulp is mixed with plenty of water.

(e) Then cellulose fibres float on the surface.

(f) Floating fibres are removed and are beaten to broken in shorter pieces.

(g) Mixture is taken in big special vats (a big sheeve to hold the pulp).

(h) It is shaked with sufficient care and craftmanship.

(i) The mixture is spread on the vat in such a manner that the fibres get distributed evenly all over the area in almost equal thickness.

(j) After the pulp is properly distributed and sufficiently dried the deckles are removed and after removing the sheet, the same is placed on felt bed with utmost care and covered with another felt sheet.

(k) In this way, sheets are placed one above another and allowed to dryup slowly in air. As they go on drying, the sheets becomes more and more smooth.

(l) When fully dried, sheets are cut to required sizes and some type herbal adhesive materials are applied on the surface to make it more suitable for writing so that ink do not spread or smudge/smear on the surface.

This method continued till nineteenth century. In 1797, paper technician Nicholar Louis Robert first invented a machine to produce paper.

1807 — Cookwerthy first used China clay and allied compounds to reduce translucentness of paper.

1952 — William James Barrow proved that the use of excess Chlorina, resin, alum, not properly processing pulp etc., cause faster deterioration. To remove resin from pulp instead of alum, cheaper alkali *e.g.* Magnesium bisulphate, calcium bisulphate, sodium carbonate, sodium sulphate etc. can be used very effectively. In 1980 about 25% of the total paper available in the American market was acid free quality. In 1959, paper was first commercially introduced in America.

W.J. Barrow indicated a maximum standard for non-coated chemical — wood paper which can be used for printing, *i.e.*

Size of paper – 62.5cm × 95cm (25" × 38")

Weight per ram (500 sheets) – 26.23 kgs.

1. The paper must be free of ground wood and inbleached fibres.
2. Initial folding endurance of conditioned strips shall average not less than 300 folds in the weakest direction as measured on the M.I.T. tester at ½ kgm tension.
3. After artificial aging at 100° (± 2%) the average of strips shall not show less than the following fold and tear for the days of aging indicated:

Days	Fold	Tear
12	200	53 gms
24	140	48 gms
36	100	43 gms

4. The pH of the paper shall not be less than 6.5 at time of manufacture, and after heat aging (as in 4) for 3 days shall show no sharp decline.
5. Opacity of the paper shall not be less than 90.

Royal Society of Arts (1898)

Good paper should contain —

(a) 60% alpha cellulose fibre, the quality of resin used along with normal or slighty acidic alum.

(b) Acidic alum should not be more than 1.5 per cent.

(c) Minerals used for loading should never be more than 10%.

(d) pH level of the paper produced should be at least 6 or above.

If the pulp is not processed properly, certain amount of lignin and some other materials in form of impurities remain in the pulp. Such pulp containing impurities are known as Beta-cellulose and gama-cellulose. Both depend on quantities of impurities present.

The paper made from longer fibres strong and durable and if these fibres are uniformly distributed in all directions, it becomes stronger. But in case of machine-made paper, the cellulose fibres are spread on the direction only and so it becomes less durable and comparatively weak. Different type of chemicals are applied on paper to make it suitable for use. To make paper suitable for printing or writing a mixture of calcium carbonate, China clay, chalk, titanium, salt, etc., are applied on the surface of the paper the process is known as calendering.

Humidity for paper: If the air is too humid, paper will swell up by absorbing excess humudity and this moisture reacts with various contituents of paper and may form acidity. Dump paper forms a very suitable medium on which mildew/

fungi can grow easily, resulting in brownish or blackish patches on paper. In case of art paper or other calendered papers the absorption of humidity makes the calendered surface soft and the pages get attached to each other to form solid blocks, which are impossible to separate or restore. In case of extremely low humidity paper losses its moisture and becomes brittle.

Excessive heat/sunlight: Paper or book should never be kept in direct sunlight as that exposure will make it yellowish and ultimately brittle after loosing its flexibility. Sunlight damages cellulose.

Similar damage are also caused by excessive heat or exposure to strong artificial light. In areas where both summer and winter are extreme paper gets easily damaged and brittle due to contraction and expansion.

20.2 Air-borne Gases

Paper is deteriorated by the presence of various pollutants in the environment. The urban air contain appreciable quantity of sulphur dioxide which reacts with moisture and oxygen present in air to form sulphuric acid, which has serious damaging effect on paper and allied materials.

In favourable conditions paper absorbs oxygen from air from cellulose compounds which react with acids resulting in breakdown of cellulose fibres into small pieces making it less flexible and brittle. This type of reaction is most common in the mechanical wood/chemical wood paper of modern time.

The most damaging result of pollutant air is acidity. The increase of acidity in paper is directly proportionate to increase in humidity and temperature. Once a paper becomes acidity for one reason or the other, it should be treated in such a manner that the acidity is neutralised and its durability is increased. The method is known as 'Deacidification of paper'.

20.3 Dust, Dirt, Smoke

Various air-borne solid particles are broadly known as dust, dirt etc.

These particulars cannot make much damage to paper directly. But its presence expedite fungal attack, acidity etc., in paper. It also effect cleanlyne of the library resulting in insect attack. Dirty spots and marking appears on paper. Small silica particular present in air effects the smoothness of paper due to abrasion.

20.4 Bacteria/Viruses etc.

Several types of air-borne bacterial and viruses reacts with iron components present in paper, resulting in appearance of brownish spots on paper surface, which is known as 'Foxing'. On careful examination it will be found that in these brownish area acidity is developed rapidly.

Fungi

Spores of fungi are always present in air. In favourable conditions, spores germinate on paper. Fungi damages cellulose for their own nourishment and growth. Comparatively moist and darker environment help quicker and extensive growth of fungi. Such attack makes paper weaker and leaves gray or blackish patches on it. It grows much when humidity is above 70% and most when it reaches 90% and the temperature is between 25°C and 38°C. To remove its effect proper ventilation and loose shelving of books is very useful. Artificial heat may also drive these away. Hetherington has recommended the solution —

Thermo crystals (100 grams), mercuries bichloride (4 grams), ether (200 cc) and benzene (400 cc)

The solution is poisonous and inflammable and must be used very cautiously. It is best applied in open air or in a well ventilated room and with a piece of cotton held in forceps so as to keep it off one's hands.

20.5 Silver fish

It is a very strange insect as it hides away in the clay and makes the binding, paper and starch its prey at night. This can be recognized as having silver grey scale on the body. Glue, paste and gelatin attract these insects. Cleanliness is a permanent cure. But these can be repelled if a mixture of simple boric acid and flow are spread near the books. A mixture of sodium fluoride and flour in the ratio of 12 : 100 would be effective for dealing with these insects.

Open access is the best prevention against all the above mentioned ills. In regions into which reader go often, the books are constantly handled and injurious organisms do not find harbour. Black colour should be avoided in the covering materials of the buildings. Red colour has proved to attract insects least.

Library's internal arrangements to check deterioration of paper

The first and foremost step to check deterioration is to effectively control the environment inside the library. The remedy is proper air conditioning. First the air with controlled humidity and temperature is allowed to pass through wire meshes (where air-borne solid particles, *e.g.* dirt, dust etc. are eliminated) and then through alkaline water.

The acidity gases and such other materials are neutralised by this alkaline solution. The pH level of the solution should be remain between 8 to 9. The temperature within the library should be controlled between 20° to 25°C and relative humidity around 45 per cent, as at that condition the element, in the air causing acidity remain least effective.

REFERENCES

Borrow, W.J. "Paper" *Library Conservation Powder*. Hutchinson, 1983.

Dasgupta, K. *Conservation of Library Materials*. Calcutta, Nation & Lib., 1988.

Fox, L.L. "A Two-year Perspective on Library Preservation." *Lib. Res. & Tech. Services* 30, 3, 1989.

Longstroth, K.E. "The Preservation of Library Materials." *Lib. Res. & Tech. Services* 3, 33, 1989.

Sharma, C.K. *Dictionary of Library & Inf. Science*. Delhi, 2002.

Sharma, C.K. *University Library: Management and Organization*. Delhi, Metropolitan, 1977.

Watt, M.A. "The Preservation of Library Material." *Lib. Res. & Tech. Services* 36, 3, 1992.

21

NATIONAL LIBRARY SYSTEM

Government of India has always been encouraging and taking steps to develop libraries in Indian territory.

1st Step: National Library (Indentures Validation) Act, 1902 in which all the books and property of several libraries taken over to enrich the Imperial Library and make it serviceable to the public.

2nd Step: National Government took serious steps to establish a library at National level as per Notification of Gazette of India (1902) in which aims and objects of a National Library were formulated.

3rd Step: Union Government decided to make the library at use to the public and hence started reading room.

4th Step: The next step was the Delivery of Books & Newspaper Act (1954) (amended in 1956).

5th Step: Because of huge collection the National Library was divided in 3 parts (Libraries) —

1. National Copyright Library.
2. National Dormitory Library
3. National Service Library.

21.1 National Copyright Library

Books received under Delivery of Books Act will not be lent out to any but a court of law.

Books will not be given for consultation in the premises of the library till the expiry of 10 years of its publication.

21.2 National Dormitory Library

Books needed out by any of the libraries, should be preserved in this library.

It house rare and out of print book. This library provide service for research and Bibliographic purpose.

21.3 National Service Library

1. Documents of current value and in fair frequent demand.

2. A state service library will be automatically formed under National Service Library programme. Multiple National service library system is adopted in Denmark, USA and UK.

21.4 Indian National Library

ALA Glossary: "A library maintained by a nation".

Unesco Symposium on National Library in Europe —

"National library of a country is the one responsible for collecting and conservation the whole of country's book production for the benefit of future generations".

A National library is a library which is a centre of collection of books and similar material organized and administered for reading, consultation and study.

According to Symposium on National Library in Europe organized by UNESCO, Vienna 8-27 Sept. 1958

In this symposium the following proposals were approved:

1. Specialization of librarianship.
2. There should be common catalogue and bibliographical rules.
3. National library should be of Encyclopedic character.
4. Latest methods should be applied like Punch cards by Automation, microcopying etc.
5. There should be a provision of equipment of exhibition, lecture room and mobile microfilming.
6. There should be a set-up of 'International Centre for the study of the preservation and restoration of cultural property' under Unesco's auspices to provide documentation and giving advice.

7. National library should work as National Bibliographical Information Centre.

IFLA: International Federation of Library Association organised three symposium and recommended to establish —

(a) National & Universal library section.

(b) Commission on Union Catalogue and International Loan Exchanges.

(c) Commission on Professional training.

History: The first step towards the establishment of National library was that there was a Calcutta Public Library. Mr. J.H. Stockqueler (editor of Englishmen) stressed for the establishment of a Public Library of reference and circulation.

A Provisional Committee of 24 perons was appointed to give their views about the development of a big large library.

Prince Dwarika Nath Tagore was the first proprietor of Calcutta Public Library and a building was constructed for Rs. 68,000 only.

There was a collection of 4675 books donated by Lord Metcalfe, Governor General on the conditions —

(a) Society will provide place and fittings,

(b) Government appoint an examination committee to see the working of the library.

In 1836 the library was established at Fort William.

In 1841 the library shifted to Metcalfe Hall, which was a building of East India Company.

In 1830 — 1846 this was the only library but in 1850 May, the Municipal Public Library were established in the city.

A subcommittee was appointed in 1873. This committee was given responsibility to review the working of the existing public library and suggest a plan for its development.

Mr. M.A. Mackangie submitted a plan of re-organization of the library to the Government. He suggested that library should be converted as Municipal library and opened to public free of cost.

Other suggestions were —

(a) to convert to municipal library,

(b) to provide free lending,

(c) to appoint a committee consisted:

(1) Six Nominees of Municipality.

(2) 4 elected representations of proprietors.

(3) 2 Government nominees.

(d) Timings should be from 10 a.m. to 5 p.m.

The above committee was the result of the visit of Lord Curzon, who appointed in 1873 the committee to go in the working of the library. The Municipal library was in miserable condition.

There was a Imperial library constituted by the merger of various secretariat libraries. Lord Curzon amalgamated both the libraries — Calcutta Public Library and the Imperial library in 1891. At that time there were 40000 volumes and total expenditure incurred upto that date was Rs. 2,50,000.

The condition of amalgamation was —

(a) Payment of shares @ 500 each.

(b) Proprietors allowed facilities for use of Imperial library.

(c) Books not required by Imperial library will be returned to council of Calcutta Public Library.

In 1902 The Governor General submitted a bill of Imperial library which was passed as Imperial Library Act, 1902 (I of 1902).

The act made provisions that —

1. Persons will hold reading tickets.
2. Reading tickets will be issued to the persons above the age of 18 years.
3. It worked as Reference library and not to home study.
4. Timings – 10 a.m. to 7 p.m.
   Sunday – 2 p.m. to 5 p.m.

Librarians

Ist Librarian (1903) - Mr. Hohn Mc Farlane of British Museum

2nd Librarian	-	Shri Hari Nath De, a linguist. He was In-charge of the library in 1906 and remained for four years.
3rd Librarian	-	J.A. Chapman — 1911-1930
4th Librarian	-	K.M. Asudulla — 1931-1947.
5th Librarian	-	V.S. Keshvan — 1948-1962 National Library
6th Librarian	-	Y.M. Mulley — 1963-1967 National Library
7th Librarian	-	D.R. Kalia — 1967-Aug 14, 1970 National Library

Building

Calcutta Public Library — 1835

↓

Imperial Library — 1891

↓

(Imperial Library Act, 1902)

↓

(National Library)

1948 — Old Viceregal palace of Belvedare

1963 — New building (extension) Multistoreyed

Regional or Copyright Libraries

1. Regional National Library (Copyright libraries)	Delhi
2. Regional National Library (Royal Asiatic Library)	Bombay
3. Regional National Library (Canmera Public Library)	Madras

Canmera public library (March 2, 1890) was declared Depository library for U.N. Publication in 1955, receiving publiction in Delivery of Book Act since September 1955.

First proposal for copyright library by Richey Committee in 1926:

- Library council formed in 1931.
- Sub-committee 1932-33.
- The delivery of books (public libraries) Act was passed on 21-05-1954 and amended in 1956 to include Newspapers and periodicals.
- Children library – Jan. 22, 1960 restricted to the age 5-12.

Organizational setup

Divisions and Sections

The organization was formed in 1969.

1. Acquisition Section
2. Cataloguing Section-I
3. Cataloguing Section-II
4. Bibliography and Reference Division
5. Reading Room
6. Lending Section
7. Stack and Book binding Division
8. Administration Division.

Service Divisions

1. Technical Service Division (Eng.)
2. Technical Service Division (Non-English)
3. Readers Service Division
4. Indian Language Division
5. Asian and African Service Division
6. Bibliographical Service Division
7. Documentation Service Division
8. Reprographic and Printing Division
9. Auxilliary Service Division
10. Fold Service Division
11. Administrative Service Division

Personnels

1. Director
2. Jt. Director

3. Dy. Directors
4. Officers of the Deptts.
5. Head of Divisions

Council of the National Library

2 members nominated by Govt. of India

2 members nominated by Govt. of West Bengal

1 member nominated by University of Calcutta

1 member nominated by Central Universities

4 members nominated by State Govts.

Ex-officio Secretary — Librarian/Director

Chairman = Jt. Education Advisor (Culture)
(Ministry of Education).

Special Features

1. It is an institute of National importance.
2. Its obligation is to collect, preserve the total national cultural output.
3. It should disseminate knowledge at a national level.
4. It should lead to the other libraries in the country in matters of planning techniques and organization.
5. It should make rare and out of print works and MSS available to various libraries in reproduced forms.

Functions

1. Maintenance of collections of all document publish within the country and also foreign publications.
2. Serving as depository library for government documents and publications received under the Copyright Act.
3. Preparation of National bibliography.
4. Providing services under Inter-library loan between Indian and foreign libraries.
5. Doing extensive cataloguing and classifications.
6. Maintenance of Union catalogue of all the libraries of the countries.
7. Service to the local populations.

8. Service to special type of readers — blinds and sea farers.
9. Technical help to other libraries.
10. Maintenance of contact libraries abroad.
11. Co-operation with International organization and bodies.
12. Reference service at National and International level.
13. Preparation of subject and other types of bibliography and documentation.

Dr. S.R. Ranganathan suggested the following Library System

3 National Central Libraries

1. National Copyright Library
2. National Dormitory Library
3. National Service Library

1. National Copyright Library

In this library books are received under Delivery of Books Act. The books are not lent out to any reader except the court of law. Books are not given for consultation in the premises of the library till the expiry of 10 years of its publications.

2. National Dormitory Library

Books weeded out by any of the libraries should be preserved in this library. Rare and out of print books are preserved in this library. This library is used for bibliographical purposes.

3. National Service Library

All current volumes are kept in this library, which are of current value and in fairly frequent demand. It is a service library where any national can read and lent out the books for home reading, but under limited cases and under full precautionary bylaws. This library is mostly provide Inter-library-loan service to the National and international libraries.

Under National Service library programme state libraries are formed in every state which are service capsules of National Library but under the administration of the state.

21.5 Types of National Libraries

1. National library of general character (Under Public Library System)
2. National special library specialised in specific subjects.
3. National library for special types of documents
4. National library for special type of readers.
5. National copyright libraries.
6. National library providing special type of services.
7. National library for special languages.

Example

1. National Library of India (Calcutta)
2. Indian Science Library (Bangalore)
3. National Archives (Delhi)
4. National Library for visually handicapped (Dehradun)
5. National Copyright Library
6. INSDOC (Documentation Service)
7. Hindi Nideshalay Library.

REFERENCES

Burse, G.V. "Co-operation Acquisition." *Lib. Jrl.* 78, 1969.

Goadrum, C.A. *Library of Congress.* New York, Praeger, 1975.

Mount, H.E. "Planning for Special Library." *Spl. Lib. Asso.*, 1972.

Rechardon, E.C. "The National Library Problem Today." *Lib. Jrl.* XXXX, 1965.

Verma, S.E. *National Library & Inf. System.* Jaipur, Prentice Hall, 1985.

22

ACADEMIC LIBRARIES

22.1 Explosion of Knowledge

It is an era of 'knowledge explosion'. On the other hand it is also called the era of "Information crisis". On the analogy of the modern trend of calling the problems faced by the society by the terms such as food crisis, energy crisis, population crisis etc. Knowledge or information, is so vital for the progress of humanity and well-being of a nation or society and is popularly expressed by the phrase "Knowledge is Power" that the wave front of knowledge is expending with a tremendous speed. It is becoming increasing difficult for an individual scientists or research worker or specialist to keep himself informed of the latest thought created in his field in any part of the world.

The factors responsible for knowledge explosion:

1. Science and technology is advancing steadily through more than five orders of magnitude.
2. The population of scientists and engineers in the developing countries has been increasing at an average of 2.5 per cent which is higher than the rate of growth of world population.
3. The universities and institutions of higher learning are switching over to seminars, symposia, project works, group discussions and ultimately multi-phased research activities and started having close liaison with industries and industry biased research is in progress in various departments.

Scientists and Information Explosion

The present situation of down pour of knowledge has

created a dilemma in the minds of research workers and scientists whether to get along with has own work unmindful to what has been done elsewhere and be unperturbed to spend his time in document search or contrary to this he may devote the necessary time and energy in pursuing the current literature on his field and making a thorough search.

As a joint venture of Librarians, bibliographers, documentalists, information scientists and information officers throughout the world information dissemination centres both at governmental levels as well as non-governmental and private levels are being set up on the lines suggested by UNISIST, UNESCO and agencies like NATIS, INIS, CODAT (Paris), NTIS, NISSAT, INSDOC, VINITI etc. are being set up in different countries. These centralized information dissemination agencies have also set up data banks and are making extensive use of modern electronic devices such as computers — Information is stored on magnetic tapes, magnetic discs, magnetic drums, micro fishes, micro cards etc. and is retrieved by means of mechanical and electronic devices.

22.2 Academic Library and Social Change

What is true of universities is equal true of their surrogates, including the libraries attached to them. They confine their service to the chosen few who, thanks to our social structure, get themselves placed in the privileged positions.

Public libraries are few, people with a strong urge to acquire knowledge still fewer, and those with the capacity and willingness to buy books almost absent. These socio-economic factors place special responsibilities on our university libraries to think of venturing into areas which are conventionally thought to be outside their purview. Libraries do not grow in vacuum, they function in societies. Their functions are determined by social forces. As social conditions change, so do the library functions.

The library is amongst all the institutions, the most adopt to changing situations. It is the most flexible institution to be shaped into the patterns most appropriate to its varying clientele. There is no individual or group that does not have a claim to the international and educational services of a library.

Library service to the community should exhibit all the characteristics of a co-ordinating structure that is so desperately needed for planned social and individual change. No doubt, the effectiveness of a university library will be magnified if it is part of a national regional network of libraries and related information services. Possible a system in which administratively the university libraries form part of the university set-up, but extend some of their common services and start special services for the select public, may fill up some of the present gap between university libraries and the community.

Services performed by university libraries are:

1. A organization of all kinds of reading material, selected and acquired, for convenient use through a helpful self-arrangement, classification and cataloguing;
2. Lending of reading material;
3. Provisions of information service to locate facts and references needed for day-today work, or, for long range research project;
4. Guidance to readers in efficient use of library resources; and
5. Display and publicity of acquisitions in order to further stimulate their use by a large body of readers.

University libraries to a great extent satisfy the specialized and research demands of certain members of the community unconnected with university, but engaged in intellectual and scholarly pursuits, by extending to them common services like seating facilities, restricted lending of reading material, current awareness service, selective dissemination of information service etc.

University library may prepare a profile of the leading persons, including the concerned government officials, in the capital interests in the study of their areas and send to them on regular basis information of their interest on special occasions the library may organize exhibition of reading material for the occasion and open the exhibition for the whole public, publicising in advance the occasion in leading newspapers.

The library may arrange on a regular basis special lectures and concerts and invite specialists to speak to the public on topics of general interest.

Libraries are agencies that reflect the social milieu to a certain degree, responding in various measures, to the changing trends in the social, economic, educational, technological and cultural environments of a country. Libraries are also potential instruments of social change, although this potentiality has not been fully explored, much less explored.

Almost all institutions and organizations — educational, professional, social, cultural, technological etc. have been concentrated incites and libraries have grown around them.

Another important aspect of academic library that will have for reaching effect on libraries is the recognition of the pervasive and vital role of information for educational development. The international approach to information through UNISIST and the activities of other international organizations like UNIDO, UNDP, IAEA, FAO and others programming and funding of library and information services and the expanding activities of ASLIB, the NISSAT and NIC programmes of our own country are just a few evidences to substantiate the recondition of the present role of information.

The application of technology in developing the information network will be the most important factor. In most of the industrially advanced countries computer technology, reprographies and miscrographies and telecommunication technology have been revolutionising the whole information transfer process. Several hundreds of computerised bibliographical data-bases, are today available online. Computer software packages for information retrieval and for computerising several library operations are now available on commercial basis. Unesco has offered the ISIS (Integrated Set for Information Services) package for the installation of computerised information services in developing countries. Technology has indeed opened new avenues for experimentation in the library and information field.

Library education at all levels should be provided in developing countries wherever and whenever the country can support these activities. Libraries are one of the most effective means of making the materials of education available to all people; they have an essential role to play in the cultural, economic and social progress of every nation, state and community.

A primary goal was the accumulation and preservation of large collections of books and research materials of Indian origin in India for the use of Indian schools. The passage of the Delivery of Book Act was one such action which paved the way for the acquisition of Indian material in more than one centre.

22.3 Clientele

There are mainly 2 types of clientele in academic libraries *i.e.* the already motivated readers *i.e.* faculty members, research scholars and scientists which are very well aware with the library, its use in their particular field of activities. This is done by librarian/information officers at their own level.

The cater to the information needs of the next category "to be motivated" who are not aware and needs awareness, guidance and help of the librarians and the information scientists.

22.4 Changing Concept of University Libraries

Libraries were thought in the earlier days as mere unavoidable necessities, asides, appendages, or ornaments. There was not much of relevance between what was collected in the university and college libraries in those days and the teaching and research programmes prevailing then. There were the days when education was more or less teacher centred and research activities were carried on rarely and in few selected activities by few research workers. It was an era of solo research. The responsibility of the universities in those days was limited to a mere supervision of what was going on in the affiliated colleges and to conducting the annual examinations. The teaching programmes were limited to a handful of subjects in the humanities and the social sciences.

"Education for all", became the slogan of modern era. In India the nationalist movement also became more vigorous and there was a gradual awakening all over the country.

With the advent of Independence, India after centuries of alien rule, found herself in the grip of a multitude of problems — economic, political, social and cultural. There was a phenomenal growth in the number of schools, college and universities. The number of universities rose from a mere 27 in 1947 to over a hundred in 1976. With the establishment of the U.G.C. in 1955 and with Dr. C.D. Deshmukh assuming its Chairmanship in 1956 a new era in the development of university education started in India and number of universities raised to 210 in 1996. Libraries which had been relegated to a secondary position and had been playing a very passive role in the teaching and research programmes on the university campuses began receiving the attention and importance due to them. Everywhere now independent library buildings started coming up and the book collections burgeoned. The collections that were built up were responsive to the needs of the teachers, the students and the research workers. Education became both teacher centred and library centred, and in the research programmes the emphasis shifted from also research to team research and even relay-research.

The success of a library system is measured by the number of satisfied users and with all the phenomenal development that has taken place in university libraries in India during the last two decades or so, it has been daily realised that the number of satisfied users is now on the decline, the main reason being that while their demands have steadily gone of multiplying, the funding has gone on becoming slenderer and thinner.

22.5 Service to Researchers and Teachers

The University Grant Commission had encouraged some years ago a scheme whereby teachers in the universities and college were encouraged to build up their personal libraries. Some universities did implement the scheme. If this scheme is extended to all the universities as a matter of course, the personal libraries of teachers are sure to reduce the strain on the university libraries of acquiring books constantly required by teachers and students to a considerable extent for which librarians should maintain profiles of the research workers, and render SDI and other services tailored to their requirements.

The problem of funds will however continue to bother Indian University libraries. The reader in a particular university library must have the feeling that once he enters the portals of his library he is, as it were, entering the portals of all the university libraries in the country at the same time. Contrast this need of the hours with a situation which existed only about a decade ago. University libraries now, are, by and large, without any let or hindrance, lending books to sister university libraries; even then the situation needs a vast improvement.

22.6 Higher Education and Academic Library

Proper libraries with adequate library facilities and competent library service are in the *sine qua non* of pulling up quality of education. But the constraint of resources require selection of programmes which would give full money value for financial investments made. "The effort should be to meet the demand for additional facilities in regular institutions, and also through correspondence courses and private study".

Every efforts should be made to challenge and stretch the minds of the students by assigning them more exacting reading assignments asking them to solve more difficult problems and providing opportunities for independent study of subjects in which they become especially interested. In addition, the students should be encouraged to do much more general reading than they do at present, both during the academic year and in vacation period.

22.7 Teaching Methods and Library

Thinking on methods of teaching by 'lecture and text-book' is changing. "If one of the main purposes of university education is to teach students to work on their own, reading by students must be preferable to attendance at a lecture unless the lecture is superior in presentation or content to the available literature". This demands for the provisions of well-stocked and well-maintained libraries. Considering the crucial importance of libraries for developing education and improving the quality of education it is right that in France, University Libraries is the responsibility of National Ministry of Education.

Outside the Central Library of a University, there are other smaller libraries working in the campus (i) Departmental Libraries that is libraries located in University teaching departments of different subjects (ii) textbooks libraries (iii) non-textbook libraries for undergraduates (iv) college libraries (v) teacher's personal library. These libraries function well on account of easy accessibility of teacher's guidance and supervision, ready availability books on specialized subjects or particular topics on specialized subjects, informal environment and no working hours limitations.

22.8 Textbook Libraries

Textbooks need not be restricted to the confines of subject-proper. In view of the interdisciplinary approach to study, the concept of textbooks will have to be widened so as to cover relevant material of allied topics on the subject. Further, a textbook treatment of the entire subject matter may not be of the same high standard. So the teacher will have to select reading material from different chapters covering the entire syllabus of a course. So properly speaking there could be a number of textbooks on a subject, unlike early nineties, when one textbook sufficed. Hence it is necessary that there should be textbooks available for study to the students which he has not to purchase or cannot purchase. Multiple copies of the textbooks should be available in the textbook libraries or study centres. Textbook service should not be applied in university library. Even if it is necessary it should be separate from the reference and research collection.

22.9 Library and the Medium of Education

In India we have adopted regional languages as medium of education. But English as an important library language continues and would continue to play a vital role in higher education. It has effected the use of library English books and journals lying unused in many libraries since the major part of library grants is spent on books and journals written in English. It is also very difficult to find source material in regional languages particularly in the research books and research journals.

The Education Commission recommends, "No student should be considered as qualified for a degree, in particular, a master's degree, unless he has acquired a reasonable proficiency in English (or in some other library language)". Thus there is a necessity that all teachers should be essentially bi-lingual so that they would be able to teach in regional language and in English.

Current academic opinion now strongly advocates the self-education or informal education. The education will have to shift its emphasis from imparting knowledge to inculcating habits of self-help and self-study. The increasing switch over the non-lecture method of teaching demands the stocking of a number of copies of given reading material. Also by persuasion the velocity of circulation of reading material has to be improved. Reading habit has to promoted in our students.

22.10 University Libraries in India

The objectives of a university library are to meet the literature requirements concerned with teaching, research and other academic programme of the university. The public of the university library is heterogeneous, as it has to cater to the requirements of persons of different tastes and levels. The purpose of the university library is to support the university's total programme. The objectives of the university libraries are to (1) acquire and accumulate varied nature of use material to meet the needs of different levels of users (2) to arrange the essential reading material and other library (3) to guide research scholars and provide them the resources useful for advancement of their research projects (4) to keep the faculty members informed of the nascent thoughts in their fields of specialization and also of the all-round developments in the society (5) to inform the authorities about the achievements and literary output of the university and to seek financial support for the development.

There has been a vast change in the shape and service of libraries during last two decades. Many university libraries have been placed in magnificent big buildings, huge grants have been made available, large number of professional and non-professional staff have been employed and large number of users are visiting these than ever before.

22.11 University Library System in India

The primary aim of university education is to cater the needs of those who are interested in higher education and those who want to spread their knowledge in the interest of nation and society. A university mainly stands for higher learning and research. It means a university must have more post-graduate course, it must provide the resources to research scholars and should be empowered to provide graduate degree, post-graduate degree in more than one subject and doctoral degrees in various disciplines.

The first library at Bombay University was founded by the donation of Premchand Roy of a sum of rupees four lakhs in 1884, the second in the line was Calcutta University Library in 1873. In 1882, the Hunter Commission was appointed to evaluate the working conditions of libraries and library system. The Government Resolution (1913) on Educational Policy accepted the need for establishing a few more universities. This resolution felt the need to restrict the jurisdiction of existing universities and suggested to establish a separate university for each of the leading provinces and to create new local teaching and residential universities within each of the provinces. As a consequence of these efforts, in between 1913 to 1921, six new universities came into existence. A residential university was established at Lucknow in 1920. The Banaras Hindu University, Varanasi, founded by Pandit Madan Mohan Malaviya, in 1916 and the Aligarh Muslim University, Aligarh, founded by Sir Syed Ahmed Khan in 1920. In the meanwhile two princely states like Mysore and Hyderabad also established universities in 1916 and in 1918 Osmania University, respectively. In 1920, with the introduction of Montford Reforms, the universities felt the necessity to establish the teaching and research departments, and consequently several universities started to provided the teaching and research facilities. After 1921, when education was transferred to Indian control, the development of universities was much faster and during the next 5 years, the number has reached to 210.

22.12 Education Commissions and Libraries

In order to improve the conditions of libraries and to render the better library services to its users many education commissions were appointed by the Government of India, after independence. The first Education Commission, was appointed by the Government of India, in 1948, known as Radhakrishnan Commission. The Commission reviewed all the aspects of education and libraries and made necessary recommendations for admission, control, finance, various facilities and courses, research projects and the need of establishing the well organized libraries. The Commission recommended: the introduction of open access system in university libraries, increasement of library hours, beyond to the college or university hours; organization and creation of new large libraries; and need of having adequate and well-qualified staff in hierarchy. It also recommended that 6¼% of total budget or Rs. 40 per student should be spent on libraries, and also recommended to introduce a non-recurring grant once in every five years.

The University Grants Commission was constituted in 1953. In 1956 by an act of Parliament, it was given an autonomous statutory status. This was a landmark and turning point in the history and development of university libraries. Since its inception, the UGC is regularly providing appropriate grants and funds to all universities for development of libraries, to purchase books and journals. The UGC is also providing grants for construction of new library buildings and for library equipment and furniture. In 1957, the Commission appointed a library committee under the Chairmanship of Late Dr. S.R. Ranganathan. The Committee advised the Commission on all the aspects of libraries.

In July 1964, another Education Commission was appointed by the Government of India under the Chairmanship of Dr. D.S. Kothari to evaluate the entire conditions of education and so also the libraries. The commission suggested that each university should develop a well-equipped library in accordance with the needs of its users.

22.13 Departmentalization

Departmentalization is clearly related with the division of labour, the span of control, and the hierarchy. It is a grouping of homogenous activities under and administration. Even the Aristotle said that if a state is large, it should be divided among many persons. Departmentalization is ordinarily thought for the major activities of the library in acquisition, preparation and the use of material. It is a primary function of a library to make books and persons advisory services available to its readers.

DEPARTMENTALISATION

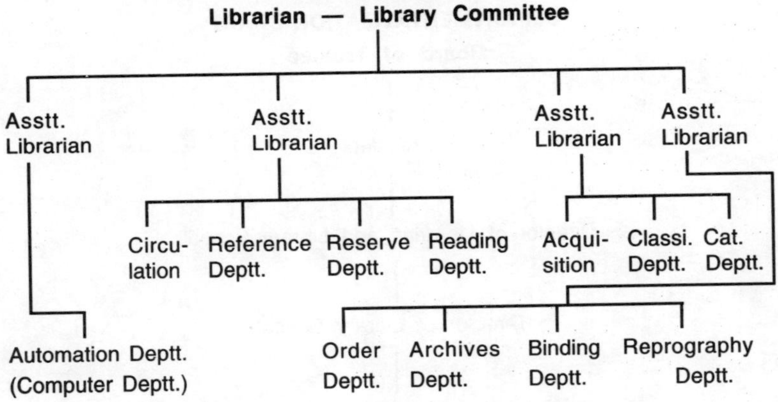

There are several system of grouping or departmentalization or sectionalization in his libraries. Important are service sections, technical sections, and material section. Willoughly has stated that departmental systems the natural outgrowth of the need of the division of labour in administration and becomes acute when the functions of an enterprize multiply over and over.

Indian National Library

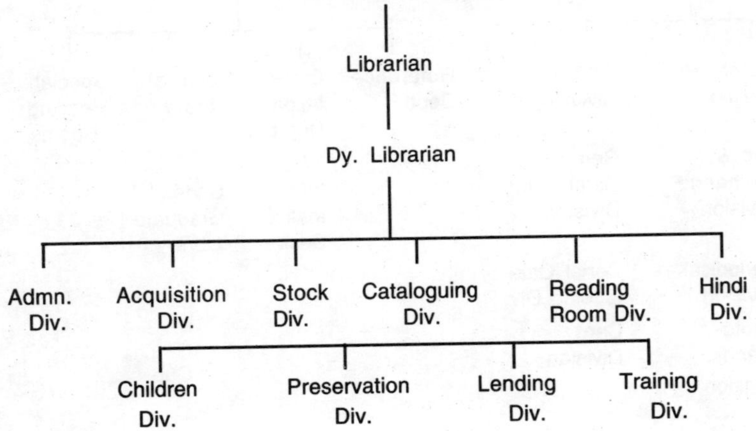

Tauber has divided the functions of a University Library into two main divisions:

1. Technical Section
2. Service Sections

DEPARTMENTALIZATION CHART

Board of Trustee

- President
  - Director of Libraries and Library School
    - Director of Library School
      - Asstt. Librarian for Personnels
        - Administrative Assistant
          - Associate Director for Technical Departments
            - Purchase Division
            - Gift & Exchange Division
            - Periodical Division
            - Photo-graphic Division
            - Binding Division
            - Gen. Cataloguing Division
            - Serial Cata-loguing Div.
            - Card Division
          - Associate Director for Public Service Departments
            - Reference Deptt.
            - Circu-lation Deptt.
            - Infor-mation Desk
            - Deptt. at Library
            - Under Graduate Library
            - Special Reading Rooms

Tauber has determined the responsibility of Technical section such as cataloguing, binding, classification and photography services. He categorised the departments as under:

Acquisition Deptt. – Acquisition, cataloguing, classification, binding, and photography.

Service Deptt. – Reference, circulation, information desk, and departmental libraries.

There is no uniform pattern of departmentalization in his libraries. The variations are effected by the traditional, personal, physical arrangements, financial availability, curriculum, type of collection, the personality and attitude of library authorities. Department should be generalised on preferential basis if local variables are not involved. University library decides its departments based on its functions and faculties.

22.14 Academic Library and Modern Trends in Researches

There are three basic questions that evaluation seeks to answer:

1. Where are we going (direction)
2. How for have we gone? (output)
3. How efficiently have me done own job (cost benefit evaluation).

The first of the above questions refers to the assessment of the certain programmes meant to benefit the society *i.e.* Library service. The second question refers loan assessment in physical terms *i.e.* reading material. The third question relates to the assessment whether the actual benefits accrued from a research programme *i.e.* reader's satisfaction.

Purpose: The scientific research is a systematic, controlled, empirical and critical investigation of hypothetical propasions about the presumed relations among natural phenomenon.

Research programming is a trinity of:

1. *Planning*: It includes history the hypothesis and their operational implications to the final analysis of the data.
2. *Structure*: It is a outline, the scheme, the diagram of the operation of the variables.

3. *Strategy*: It includes the methods to be used to collect and analyse the data.

The library is now a necessity unit in social fabric. Books are one social mechanism for preserving the racial memory and the library one social apparatus for transferring this to the consciousness of living individuals. Thus Librarianship takes its place among the phenomena to be discussed in any system of social sciences. Science means systematic and formulated knowledge, the knowledge of universe around us. In science it becomes a matter of duty to expose a supposed law to every possible kind of verification and this is done intentionally (and not left to mere accident as in the case of apples). If there is no variation in the result of our experiments, our confidence in law is established. The Scientific research is a systematic, controlled, empirical and critical investigation of hypothetical prepositions about the presumed relations among natural phenomenon.

Modern Library is a house of information and librarian is a bypass media of information transmitted through reading material librarian perform the function of a information officer, bibliographer, helper, guide, and overall a torch bearer to a society. He is a research oriented professional who reviews the library affairs time to time and efforts to overcome the problems caused by various allied components: reading material, readers, and staff.

Schulter has suggested the following steps:

1. Selection of field, topic or subject for research.
2. Survey of the field to comprehend the research problem.
3. Developing a bibliography.
4. Formulating or define the problem.
5. Differentiating and outlining the elements and problems.
6. Classifying the elements in the problem according to their relations to data or evidence.
7. Determining the data or evidence requires.
8. Ascertaining the availability of data or evidence.
9. Testing the problems.
10. Collecting data and information.

11. Synthesizing and arranging the data preparation to their analysis.
12. Analysis and interpreting the data.

A society stagnate unless it makes constant provision for the injection and absorption of new knowledge which is best done through the library. Formal education is definitely mere expensive than non-formal education. So most of the expectations of newly emerging socio-economic group for higher education will be largely met by informal education. Academic libraries should be organized, developed, and administered with objectives in accordance with objectives which inculcate reading habits and help in research development reflecting the specific needs and aims of the nation.

"Every effort should be made to change and stretch the minds of the researchers by assigning them more exactly reading assignments asking them to solve more difficult problems and providing opportunities for independent study of subjects in which they become especially interested". The character and efficiently of academic institution may be gauged by its treatment of its central organ — the library.

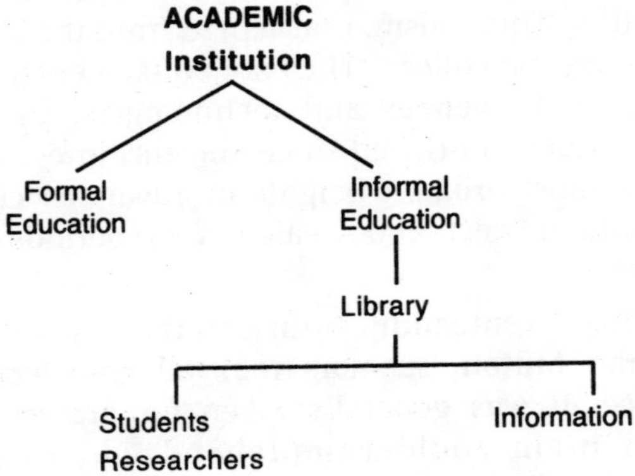

22.15 Research Services

Academic libraries extend their services to the academic community in following fields of services:

1. Academic library displays the reading material, selected and acquired for convenient use through a helpful

self-arrangement systematic classification and cataloguing.

2. It provides reading material through its lending services to the researchers.
3. It makes necessary provisions of information services with a view to locate facts and references needed for day to day work, or for long range research projects through current awareness service and selective dissemination of information.
4. It guides the readers and explorate its resources to the maximum use of library potentiality.
5. It provides bibliographical services in the specific field of researches on demand or offer.

22.16 U.G.C. Contribution

U.G.C. has continuously made efforts to make the higher education research oriented. It has encouraged interdisciplinary researches. UGC has liberally granted financial assistance to short-term and long-term researches and simultaneously liberal grants to libraries to provide necessary research material to the researchers.

The library has occupied a central place in an educational institution. This truism, is accepted from the largest university to the smallest college. They are equally essential to the pure and applied sciences and technologies. In various forms, libraries have flourished since ancient times. They have risen to their most brilliant heights in advanced civilizations and sunk into neglect and weakness in periods of intellectual decadence.

In the seventeenth century, in the days of Francis, Bacon and John Milton, scholars took all knowledge to be their province. It was generally taken for granted that a single human brain could comprehend and hold all existing knowledge. Today that delusion has vanished, as the arts and sciences have been broken down into more and more minute compartments and specialities. The burden of storing human knowledge has been shifted multiple reading material of various kinds and forms in libraries.

Man is different with other creature because of his characteristics and nature. Man with his vocal and written language and conversation with each other has developed his knowledge based on the learning and experience. The university library must be a dynamic, living organism, fully responsive to change and always looking to the future. It is generally recognized that the rate of technological progress is constantly accelerating. The chief effect of technology on the book world up to now, however, has been to speed production. Books, magazines, and other types or printed matter are being produced continuously. The book as we have known it since 1450 will remain the staple offering of libraries and will not be superseded by any invention simply because it is the most satisfactory, attractive, efficient and economical device ever discovered for its purpose. Further research and experimentation will result in the successful adaptation of electronic methods for international bibliographic control, greatly expediting scholars' access to their materials.

The revolution in library architecture will continue. Such concepts as modular construction to provide for greater flexibility, scientific lighting, air-conditioning, and extensive use of color, which have come into vogue for recent library buildings will create more inviting conditions than even before for work, study, and recreation in libraries. Great advances has been made in co-operative cataloguing, nationally and internationally, with general acceptance of standardized codes, agreements among national libraries of the world to share the burden of cataloguing and publications of their own countries, and co-ordination with publishers to expedite the preparation of cataloguing data.

No library, however resourceful, can self-sufficient at any time. No library can hold all the literature which is demanded by the readers. This principle is applicable among human being, and also among libraries. There has been tremendous increase in scientific and technical knowledge during the 20th century. We call it 'Knowledge Explosion'. Every book in it should be read and every reader should benefit by a library with the co-operation of other libraries.

Libraries play a vital role in the development of higher learning. They are primarily responsible for:

(a) The selection and collection of material appropriate for libraries,
(b) The preservation of the collections,
(c) The organization of the collections,
(d) The dissemination of the material or the information which it contains.

Jewett (1850) first suggested the accumulation of ster-type blocks of the catalogue of Smit Sonian Institution for other libraries for their use, but this proposal was not implemented. In 1966 Colorado Council for libraries examined the feasibility of establishing a book-processing centre to serve all states of USA. In India, Dr. Ranganathan suggested the Inter-Library loan scheme among the university libraries which begins in 1964. It is an old concept when manuscripts of Nalanda and Taxila Libraries were consulted by the readers of the various other countries. They either copied or commandered. But in 21st century science and technology has predominated the world, which resulted, in the better competition. Several research cells were established which provided a concern over the information, storage and retrieval process. Resource sharing is initially based on primarily responsibility for each library participating adequate resources, administrative capability, efficient communications, appropriate share of responsibility and attitude of flexibility and experimentation. Resource sharing assist member libraries in the selection, processing, accessioning through co-operation and co-ordination programmes.

22.17 Field of Resource Sharing

There are many aspects of libraries in which resource sharing can be effectively applied. The following are the different ways achieve maximum benefit of co-operation:

Aspects	*Resource Sharing*
(a) Acquisition work	Co-operative Acquisition programme
(b) Storage problem	Co-operative storage centres
(c) Cataloguing problems	Co-operative cataloguing
(d) Processing problems	Book processing centres

(e) Inter-Library Loan	Inter-Library Loan programme
(f) Computer service	Co-operative computer service programme
(g) Readers service	Bibliographic centres/ Documentation Centres/ Information centres

Co-operative programme is the best media of resource sharing, but it has some demerits like local autonomy, clash of personality, unproductive demands of the readers, lack of adequate funds, limitation on access, lack of space, lack of communication and incapability of equipment and procedures. However, these problems can easily be removed unless they are not associated with technological devices. Libraries in varies nature, budget and users. Their number is still increasing whereas the amount of their budget is decreasing. Thus, there is need of better understanding among the libraries through inter and inter-institutional co-operation. Resource sharing is specific mode for library co-operation among a group of libraries, work together and make best and maximum use of their storage. A co-operative system may be centralized or decentralized. Centralization offers efficiency economy and availability of full resources of system to many and other component of users, which decentralization offers quick, direct and personalised services.

22.18 Co-operative Acquisition Programme

Co-operative acquisition is an arrangement between several libraries whereby one of them, or a separate organization, purchase books for all of them in order to obtain books at a cheaper rate than is possible for individual libraries. Although academic libraries handle a wide variety of materials both print and non-print nature. Print material generally includes books, periodicals, pamphlets, documents, manuscripts, maps and charts, while non-print material includes files, microfilms, strips, data, and records, machines etc. They are stored, classified and served in different fashion. Acquisition programme involves the process of deciding selection, ordering and material access to the library.

Selection programme is considered as an organic substitute for a book selection policy. It should be based on the budget, community to be served, curriculum and past practices of the university libraries. It should consider the demand of the academicians students and academic programmes. It is obvious that an academic library cannot delimit the collection unless the teaching programme as delimited. A complete union catalogue would contain all the monographic holdings of the member libraries and convert their retrospective holding into machine-readable form. The possible exchanges of acquisitionalists catalogue cards, and bibliographies represent another form of the selective union catalogue or list. Academic libraries preferably university libraries also share non-printed resources and need a Union Catalogue of serials as the most effective criteria. Many projects were taken by INSDOC, ISC, CSI, IARB, NLAIU, ICSSR and prepared Union Catalogue of social science and scientific periodicals, serials. But they could not be continued due to unknown reasons and present work is a drop in a sea.

As regards the ordering system in a potential resource sharing programme libraries can go in the build or batch ordering by mutual agreement. So as to reduce the cost of material, a centralized order centres may be established to facilitate this step. But it is not practicable in Indian University libraries. Moreover, there is not such centres exist in India for university libraries. UGC and ICSSR are assisting for University libraries to take step in this regard but it could not be materialised. Co-operative Acquisition programme may be taken up among university libraries of India and on an international level. A regional seminar on "Library development in South Asia" held in Delhi in 1980 which recommended a National system of centralized purchase of foreign materials. Farmington plan can be taken as base of the Acquisition co-operative programme. Co-operative Acquisition may include co-operative acquisition of translations, manuscripts, historical documents, scientific reports and bibliographical publications.

It is a need of the day and a university library committee may be formed consisting of university librarians of the different libraries to decide all matters of policy and direction regarding book selection and procurement centres, allotment of area of specialization, preparation of union catalogue, withdrawal, of out of data books and staff in service training programmes.

22.19 Democratic Steps in Academic Libraries

The university librarians have taken up an unanimous stand in just a position to the well-known position of the authorities in this connection. The selected group of librarians invited to appear before the second Sen Committee were in agreement with the general consensus that has developed throughout the length and breadth of the country.

The librarians are an internal part of the academic community composed of teachers, research staff and librarians. The librarians are thus academics but not teachers in the traditional sense of the term. They are part of the academic community because the nature of jobs performed by them has essentially an academic orientation. Reference service, collection development, bibliographic organization and control are some of the significant areas in library work which have a major academic contents.

Research Functions

1. Classification
2. Subject, area and language specialization
3. Documentation
4. Bibliographical services

Teaching Functions

1. Reference service
2. Orientation courses and lecture
3. Advisory service

The following criteria are the measuring rod for academic competence:

1. Master of 'Subject matter' (Library Science) effectiveness in teaching.
2. Ability to anticipate, identify and define areas of library service; Interaction with colleagues and readers; increased competence in performance; Effective Library leadership.
3. Ability as a scholar and work as a consultant or membership as an investigating or research committee.
4. **Effectiveness of Library Service:** Interaction with the

faculty and students and active participation in community affairs.

5. **Continuing growth:** Membership and participation in professional organization; participation in the conferences, worships and seminars.

22.20 Book Prices and Academic Libraries

The continuous price rise of books is a matter concern to all librarians irrespective of the fact they manage college and University Libraries. Library librarian/managers are mostly concerned with book prices, while preparing budgets for purchasing books. Knowledge of prices become useful for allocating funds for different subjects.

Rise in book prices affects generally budgets of libraries which are in elastic. The number of acquisitions decline with rise in prices. While formulating library budgets, the knowledge of average prices of books on various subjects along with trends in price rise enable the librarian to make adequate provision so that the quality as well as quantity of books do not suffer.

Book publishing is a complex economic activity which starts with selection of a manuscript, to the cost of paper and to the credit arrangements allowed to booksellers. The price of paper has risen dramatically resulting in higher prices of books. In India, market for books is both small and to some extent inelastic. The individual market for scholarly and general books is limited because of low literacy and low purchasing power. The only market for Indian books is the institutional market or libraries. Indian Publishers have usually priced their books at three to five times the cost of production.

The adverse effects of it are being talked about on two organized sectors. One is the book-publishing sector and the other is the library sectors. Indian publishing always said all around that it has now come into a period of crisis. So far as impact on libraries is concerned, every librarian knows that he is trying to do the impossible task of stretching an inelastic budget to cover an ever growing need for more reading material in his library.

Clientele and staff are found active — the books being in active use for inspiration and education of the community around and the staff to manage the stock and regulate use to the present and future needs of their patrons. In the trinity of 'Books', 'Readers' and 'Staff', the 'Books' have always been provided precedence. The major share of the financial resources of a library is allocated to the purchase of reading material. For an integrated development of the Libraries all the three constituents are important.

For older publications also the publishers review their prices from time to time by calculating the cost at the current rate and multiplying the cost with four. A bookseller divulged his experience with foreign publications that the prices are increased in every new list of the publisher for the already published material.

In case of periodical publications that are mostly organs of some processional and learned societies, the position is happier as the subscription rates are calculated on actual costs with a nominal margin. Libraries being a welfare unit. Libraries cannot depend upon their own income as it is always meager: (i) membership fee, (ii) overdue charges. Library grants are usually of two types: recurring to meet regular requirements and non-recurring, also known as *ad hoc* grants that are neither ascertainable nor of uniform magnitude from year to year, for the uplift of libraries. There are no uniform standards as its allocation and utilization, depends upon the discretion of the Head of the institution. The detrimental impact of rise in prices of books on the development of libraries is, primarily, due to the reason that state as well as U.G.C.'s grants are not increased keeping in view the pricing mechanism of books. If we compare the intake percentage of reading material of library with the number of titles published in a year. It has been observed that literature explosion like population explosion in our society is further shrinking the financial resources of libraries and making them poorer day by day. The rise in the prices of books and the number of titles being published a year in the market are observing geometrical progression while library grant are being increased in an arithmetical progression.

23

Public Libraries

Society consists of a wide range of people who are members of a community belonging to one or other social group. The interest of knowledge of these different groups of people is very much varied according to human needs of general nature, academic nature or special nature. A library organizes the recorded knowledge or reading material or even non-book material making them available to every member of a community for use and dissemination of knowledge. The purpose of a library in modern society is to educate the community in the widest sense. Librarian must acquire recorded knowledge that is worth-while, useful and significant to the specific community he serves. The information role of the books is important in the present age which needs above all, facts and information. It is the job of the librarian working in a public library to provide facts which are food for mind that make men and women think for themselves. The librarian is an agent of communication in modern society and doles out information for the benefit of the community the library services.

The librarian is a competent leader of the community exhibiting strength of the character, intellectual curiosity, enthusiasm, vision, forceful personality, administrative ability and freedom from bias or prejudice and tradition. He is an interesting composite having many of the qualifications of a sociologist, psychologist, teacher, historian and bibliographer. The social influence of the library is tremendous in the context of great and rapid advancement of science and technology that is taking place all over the world including India.

The library provides ample opportunity for the development of correct social attitudes and unfoldment of the personality of the group, the nation and the society at large. Socialization of the public library is also necessary as the public library represents the best opportunity for self-education of majority of the adults, who do not go in for higher education beyond secondary stage. Library is the only organized social institution which fosters the reading of books. Public libraries should extend the library facilities to the masses, both literates, neoliterates and even illiterates, so that they get opportunity to gaining all the knowledge required to make them better citizens and exercise their right to vote properly and also to develop among themselves a modern mental and scientific outlook. In India, to achieve the target of cent per cent library, the library must all itself very closely with the literacy campaign both with the adults and in the school by providing reading materials to the new literate persons. Library is the only institution which provides informal education in an informal atmosphere to the newly literate, where they feel quite at home. For a nation that reads is a nation that leads. There is also need for promotion of international understanding and world peace through books in the library. As such, public libraries have an immense contribution to make in this direction.

The need of the hour is to organise public library services in a phased programme, both in urban and rural areas, through library legislation. To meet the social needs of the society, the use of the public library is an evalutionary process. Public library is informal education and that work should be taken to people on the fringe of literacy or even to non-literates where possible.

23.1 Rural Scene

Library is a social institution charged with the most enviable functions of dispensing knowledge to the ignorant and the informed alike. "Vidya-Dan" *i.e.* imparting of knowledge has been considered as the most sacred task. The main function of a library is the collection and preservation of knowledge for its dissemination to all. The libraries have changed the outmoded concept of preserving a large number of reading materials for the sake of preservation only.

The primary education is imparted in the school, educational institute and libraries supplements the education. As "A Library is a social organization, charged with the work of creating inspirations and recreations through books of the great thinkers of past and present. Establishing libraries, is an urgent need and in rural areas, where economically poor and backward people are residing." In this connection 'Rajaram Mohan Rai Foundation' is playing very important role, to start rural libraries in the country, with a population of 5 to 10 thousand. This foundation also provides financial/ books etc. help for those libraries locating in rural/backward areas.

As most of the villagers are neo-literate or illiterate, the books must be picture-books, books with broad letters etc., so that these can be read easily. Lectures should be arranged and film show should be organised to educate them about health, family-welfare, social welfare, insurance, small scale industries and other aspects of the rural development.

23.2 Adult Education

Public libraries are the best plateform of adult education. The term adult education is used to designate specially for adults. According Gresson, "Adult education" is not adult education really in simplest terms and continuing education of adults necessary to all men, if they are to fulfil their obligations and realize their highest potential as members of society, no matter at what level it begins, at what level it involve, or how it is obtained.

The public library is best media of adult education. The public libraries were brought into the picture to undertake the adult education programmes in the 19th century. Between 1850 and now the picture of adult education has changed from uniqueness of opportunity to multiplicity of opportunities. The library is a democratic institution and has an obligation to serve both the literates and illiterates.

Earlier the public libraries played a complementary role as a sister partner to the agencies engaged in the Adult education programmes. The three functions can be assigned to the public library:

1. To initiate adult education programmes, by organizing Adult Literacy School in night after people returned from their field.
2. To co-operate with the agencies engaged in such activities by supplying the appropriate reading materials.
3. To keep the literates and neo-literates as continuous users of the library-literature, etc.

An illiterate person being worried of his illiteracy and ignorance will make an attempt to see that his children gets good education and thus struggles start in his life to bring up his children. This psychological change in minds of people of rural area/village is an important feature in eradicating the percentage of illiteracy of that area. When the illiterates gets educated, the spirit of enquiry begins and they begin to try to understand the administrative aspects of the country and send proper representatives to rule the country.

It is adults who determine the policies of their educational institutions, control and the mass media, determine policy which will create the world their children will inherit. Adult education, be non-forma, education essentially like the education imparted by the libraries, in the sense that it must always be voluntary, a thing offered and accepted or rejected at will. A library is considered to be an agency of communication mainly through the recorded words. It operates fundamentally with the individual. But its aim is not only the improvement of the individual, but also the improvement of the society, of which the individual, is a part. Library is a social creation — Jesse Shera calls it a 'Social agency', as agency which is responsible for implementing the basic underlying bodies of beliefs of any society — briefly termed as its 'culture'.

Library Adult Education programme should not have a casual or intermittent approach, but should aim at a continuing, cumulative and lasting effect upon the participants. The library must undertake this kind of programme consciously and deliberately to meet some identificable community needs through the planned and systematic use of library resources.

Public library's resources and services are freely and completely available to all in the community, irrespective of age or sex group, or with differing castes or creeds. Public library materials relate to all fields of knowledge to suit the varying educational and reading interests of each community or group of people. Public library use is completely permissive and its service is geared to meet the needs of every individual adult or group of adults.

The eradication of adult illiteracy from India has constituted an important item in the programme of our national educational policy. In order to remove this tremendous drawback in the educational and cultural condition of a vast majority of our people, several literacy programmes were undertaken and organized at various levels since the inception of the Community Development Programme. Fundamental, Each One Teach One, Social Education etc.

The drawbacks of the programme is that there is no permanent agency to carry on this programme. It even lacked a definite forum. It is not surprising that there has been a mushroom growth of such agencies just to share the NAEP potluck.

The methodology of teaching is rapidly changing. It is no more considered proper to keep the teaching activities confined to the four walls of the classroom. In the modern education system, more stress is laid on self study, self learning that on the traditional lecture-based system. Thus education learning through libraries is getting popular day by day and is replacing the classroom teaching methods.

All educational preparations are examination centred and students feel contented with the cramming of a few textbooks, guides, notes, etc. even without properly understanding their contents, which seriously affect their learning and personality development. Students are rarely initiated into the rich realms of knowledge, through self study, debates, declamation contests and other constructive extra curricular activities.

In spite of the UGC, there have been no final decision on minimum norms and standards for college libraries and their services to readers. Textbooks prescribed in various subjects are not available. The UGC has done very little for the college library and their librarians. The UGC has organised in-service training workshops, seminars etc. for the working librarians to keep themselves up-to-date is applying technology service to the readers. The role of university libraries in education and research has been streamlined to a great extent through the continuous effort of UGC and the University teachers. In view of micro-specialization/research during this period of literature explosion, the modern technological equipments of photocopying, microform, microfilms, microfiche readers, audio-visual equipment, and computer network etc. to serve specific information/articles from journals for the research workers, form the *sine qua non* of University library holdings and its services. University libraries have established computer centres and are interconnected throughout the country or at least at regional level to start with, so that the shared resources availability is made possible at electronic speed to promote research in series and the colossal wastage of research in parallel is minimised. Libraries would now be required to be strengthened in term of reading material, equipment, working space and personnel.

The new educational policy lays greater stress on distance education to provide facilities to disadvantaged section of the society in order to improve their educational qualifications higher standards of education cannot be expected through this channel unless a network of good libraries is set up.

23.3 Computers in Aid of Libraries

Various types of social, developmental, financial, scientific and technical informations are gathered, processed, compiled and stored in some form or the other. The most conventional and also most convenient form so far has been in the form of books which are stored and preserved in various libraries. The libraries, are the treasure-houses of our knowledge. They exist at different levels ranging from schools, colleges and universities to National Libraries.

In the modern times communication satellites have opened up vast new areas of application. Their link up with computer systems has further expanded their potential enormously. The use of satellites has been a major development after the large scale production of the Integrated Circuits. This owes to their enormous broad-band capacities, promising manifold applications in the areas of Radio, Television, Remote sensing of the earth resources, agriculture, aviation, meteorology and last but not least education. Few years ago 'SITE' experiment was conducted by I.S.R.O., Allahabad using INSAT satellite for telecasting the educational programmes. Even since such programmes are being regularly telecast for the benefit of the students community in our country.

All computers carry out five functions: input, storage, output, arithmetic logic operation and control. The input function brings the information into internal storage by reading holes or magnetised spots on the storage media, *e.g.*, punched cards, magnetive tape, magnetic disc or magnetic drum. The place where the input data goes to be stored and where the instructions that process this data are already stored is the storage.

There are mainly three methods of storing and retrieving data, *viz.*, Sequential, Indexed and Random. In sequential (or serial) organization the information records are stored on the output medium in the same sequence as they are written to that medium. When a programme reads data from a sequential file it will get the first data item first, then the second data item and then the third etc. etc. Indexed organization is an alternative method of arranging the data. It is be used for data on direct access storage devices (discs), not magnetic tape or punched cards. The book number for a data area is called its key.

Indexed data files can also be accessed from beginning to end, reading all the records one at a time. This is called sequential access. It makes indexed files very versatile. If you want to possess most of the records, you access the files sequentially. If only a few, you use the indexes to access these records directly. Sequential data areas can only be accessed sequentially. Indexed data areas can be accessed sequentially or directly but, with direct access, there is a lot of time lost in checking through the indexes.

A common input-output device that also serves as auxiliary storage on small computers is the flexible of floppy disk. The disk-drives rotates a floppy disk on its spindle. A movable read/write head is stationed over the rotating disk. Thus we have random access to the track number, but sequential access to the sector number, within the track.

The idea of integrating the satellite link, computer system and facsimile machine with the purpose of retrieving the written or printed information in the books could be further extended by recording and storing the received video communication on a video cassette in a Video Cassette Recorder (VCR).

A quiet revolution is taking place in this field of getting on-line access to the European data-bases and data banks numbering more than 70 covering approx. 35 million references in various branches of science and technology (while the data-bases cover abstracts of the published research papers, the data banks provide factual information). This on-line Information Retrieval System (IRS) has been made available by the European Space Agency to the National Aeronautical Laboratory (NAL), Bangalore in India.